THE SNOWMAN

COLLECTORS BOOK

Louise Irvine

RICHARD
DENNIS

ACKNOWLEDGEMENTS

This book would not have been possible without the talents of Raymond Briggs, who created The Snowman and I am grateful to him for discussing his work with me and also for writing the foreword to this book. I have been interested in The Snowman since the early 1980s, when I worked for Royal Doulton, and I was delighted when Richard Dennis offered to publish the first Collectors Book on the subject.

I have had a great deal of support and encouragement from Copyrights, the licensing agency, and I would like to thank Karen Addison, Nicholas Durbridge, Linda Pooley, Diana Neal and David Robinson for giving me access to their archives and answering my seemingly endless list of questions about The Snowman. Help was also given by their overseas licensing representatives, notably Roger Berman at Copyrights Japan and Orie Miyazaki at Sony Plaza. Alex Tham at Snowman Enterprises was also very helpful in finding pieces from their archive collection and arranging photography.

Many of the designers who have interpreted Raymond Briggs' original drawings have loaned artwork and talked to me about their role in creating The Snowman merchandise. I am particularly grateful to Neil Faulkner, Peter Roberts, Harry Sales, Kevin Scully and Caroline Dadd. The manufacturers of The Snowman merchandise have provided me with background information, production details and samples for photography and I am indebted to the following individuals: Wendy Addison at Border Fine Arts; Christina Wilkie and Rhona Burns at Caithness Glass; Philip Holdcroft and Joanna James at Country Artists; Jacky Franks at International Christmas; Maxine Canon at Isle of Man Post; Joan Jones and Julie Tilstone at Royal Doulton; George Bott, Carole Baxendale and Christine Smith at Wedgwood.

Companies that have commissioned The Snowman products have assisted me with information and photographs, notably Bruce Wheeler from the Guild of China and Glass Retailers and Nick Tzimas of UK International Ceramics.

Dedicated Snowman collectors have been very helpful in providing me with information and making pieces available for photography, in particular Sally Billings, Jerome and Rhonda Hanson; and Loraine and Martin Heywood, who travelled from the UK to Japan in quest of The Snowman products.

Thanks also to Magnus Dennis for taking most of the photographs in this book and to Hideki Tanaka and Keyline Design for supplying specific shots. Illustration from *The Man* by Raymond Briggs published by Julia McCrea/Red Fox, used by permission of The Random House Group Limited. The design and production teams at Richard Dennis Publications and Flaydemouse have also been very helpful and I am very grateful for the help and support of Richard Dennis, Wendy Wort and Chrissie Atterbury.

THE SNOWMAN™ by Raymond Briggs
© Snowman Enterprises Ltd 2004
Books published by Hamish Hamilton Ltd.
Licensed by ©opyrights Group

Photography by Magnus Dennis
Production Wendy Wort
Print, design and reproduction by Flaydemouse, Yeovil, Somerset
Published by Richard Dennis, The Old Chapel, Shepton Beauchamp, Somerset TA19 0LE
© 2004 Richard Dennis and Louise Irvine
ISBN 0 903685 95 7

CONTENTS

FOREWORD
BY RAYMOND BRIGGS

The first thing I say to interviewers is, 'Don't mention the 'S' word'. A quarter of a century of talking about The Snowman is more than enough. After several hundred interviews I have shot my bolt and retired from it. The second thing I say to the unfortunate interviewer is 'Don't ask where did you get the idea from?' This applies to anything, not just The Snowman.

Usually, you will have forgotten where the idea came from, as it is so long ago. Also, picture books take so long to do that even after the one and a half to two years producing the book, you don't remember the original 'inspiration'. Also, ideas can come in a flash and be jotted down in minutes. They then have to be filed away as you are already involved in another book at the time. The Snowman was on file for six years before I started work on it, so that is now thirty one years ago.

Another reason not to ask 'Where did you get the idea from?' is because you may have cribbed it. Friends have told me there are flying snowmen in Rupert, but despite having been a lifelong Rupert fan, mainly the original Mary Tourtel version, I have never seen these flying snowmen. I wouldn't have minded admitting pinching the idea if I had seen it, but I hadn't.

I used to tell interviewers a decade or two ago, when I was still able to talk about it, that I have a childhood memory of an old black and white Film Fun comic showing two snowmen climbing over a window sill into a house. So that may have been it, I don't know. I may have invented it to shut the interviewer up.

Collecting in general is an interesting phenomenon. It would be a good subject for a PhD, but no doubt it has been done already, many times. Probably someone, somewhere has a collection of PhD theses on collecting!

Personally, I am trying to give up collecting as I feel it can become obsessional and addictive. In my time I have collected paper knives, William books, hand-forged mattocks, electric fires, Mrs Mills LP covers and books entitled When the Wind Blows or similar (Where the Wind Blows, The Wind that Blows, When the Wind Blew, When the Wind Changes, The North Wind Blows, The Wind Blows Over, The Way the Wind Blows, A Cool Wind Blowing, So the Wind Won't Blow It All Away... etc, etc). WHY? I ask myself now. But anyway, the whole idea was spoiled by a well-meaning bookshop assistant saying that she would look it up on the internet for me. She then sent me six A4 sheets filled with titles. All the fun went out of it.

Now, aged seventy, and with the approach of intellectual maturity, I've begun to think it's all a bit daft. But it's still enjoyable and harmless, so like most collectors, I will probably go on ... and on ...

Anyone got any Mrs Mills LP covers?

Raymond Briggs at home.

THE SNOWMAN™

The Snowman has melted the hearts of collectors all over the world. From Seattle to London to Tokyo, ardent fans seek out a diverse array of Snowman products, including figures, decorative plates, musicals and trinket boxes. Even unlikely trophies, such as thermos flasks and lavatory brush holders, join displays of The Snowman memorabilia. 'Where will it all end?' cries Raymond Briggs, the artist who created this phenomenon twenty-five years ago. Never in his wildest dreams did he predict that there would be such enormous interest in his wordless tale about a little boy who builds a snowman.

RAYMOND BRIGGS

When *The Snowman* was published in 1978, Briggs was already a successful author and illustrator with several children's books to his credit. The first book to use his distinctive strip cartoon format without words was *Father Christmas* in 1973 and this won him the prestigious Kate Greenaway award for the second time in his career. The rather eccentric Father Christmas, created by Briggs, grumbles about 'another blooming Christmas' and longs for a holiday in the sun. He was loosely based on his own father, a milkman who was 'grumpy and cheery at the same time'. Briggs' choice of unconventional heroes continued in 1977 with *Fungus the Bogeyman*, which followed two years research into the putrid, boil-infested world of bogeydom in all its glorious green detail.

THE BOOK

It was a desire to produce a nice, clean, pleasant book after all the muck and slime that led Briggs to create The Snowman. It is a touching story of a little boy who builds a snowman that comes to life and they explore each other's worlds. First The Snowman investigates the boy's house and finds the fridge and deep freeze more to his taste than coal fires and central heating. After he has experimented with various domestic appliances, tried on clothes and played with toys, they take a

magical flight together over the wintry countryside, soaring over Brighton Pavilion and landing on the pier. The idea of a flying snowman seemed quite logical to Briggs, after all snow floats in the sky. Of course, snow also melts and so the story has a poignant ending when the boy awakes to find his Snowman has disappeared, leaving just his scarf and hat behind on the ground.

As Briggs explains, 'Most of my ideas seem to be based on a simple premise: let's assume that something imaginary – a Snowman, a Bogeyman, a Father Christmas – is wholly real and then proceed logically from there.' He spends months getting ideas, writing and planning before beginning to draw.

As with many of his books, Briggs introduced several personal elements. The setting is near his home in the Sussex Downs, the boy's parents are modelled on his own and the boy is an only child, just like Briggs. In the original story, the boy did not have a name but he became known as James after the film was made because there was a Christmas present addressed to him.

THE FILM

In 1982 Raymond Briggs' delightful book was turned into an animated film directed by Dianne Jackson and produced by John Coates of TVC London. The Snowman achieved superstar status when the film was nominated for an Oscar and then won a BAFTA for the best children's entertainment of 1982. Over the past twenty years, The Snowman has become essential Christmas viewing on British television's Channel 4, part of our traditional seasonal celebrations. More than two million videos have been sold for home viewing in the UK alone and it has been broadcast in over 100 other countries.

To the strains of the haunting theme song, 'Walking in the Air', composed by Howard Blake, James and The Snowman extend their flight to the North Pole for a jolly party where they meet Father Christmas and lots of new snow characters. After all this fun, the bitter disappointment when James discovers his friend has melted brings tears to the eyes of viewers, young and old. Themes of friendship, parting and loss are all explored in Briggs' original story but the film adds a new twist when James draws The Snowman scarf from his pocket – a tangible memory of a magical friendship.

THE MUSIC

'I'm absolutely amazed and thrilled my book seems to have become part of popular culture', says Briggs. He revels in the fact that The Snowman has become so familiar that there have been several comedy spoofs and that the theme tune was once voted number seven in the most hated tunes of all time. 'I cut out the list and sent it off to the composer. I'm sure he'll see the funny side of it. It's quite flattering really!' The fourteen-year-old choir boy, Aled Jones, took 'Walking in the Air' to number three in the record charts in 1985 but most people will be surprised to learn that he was not the singer in the film. Peter Auty sang in the original soundtrack but he did not have an agent to ensure his name was listed in the credits. This oversight was corrected in the 2002 version of the film. Not only can the famous theme tune be heard on videos, LPs, CDs and DVDs but most Snowman musical boxes, snow globes and key-rings play the familiar strain.

SNOWMAN ENTERPRISES

To manage the interests of this increasingly popular character, TVC formed Snowman Enterprises Ltd in 1980 with Raymond Briggs and the publishers, Hamish Hamilton. Today the General Manager, Alexandra Tham promotes and distributes The Snowman worldwide and is responsible for a regular newsletter which keeps fans up to date with new products and events. For the 20th anniversary of the film, Snowman Enterprises produced a new animated introduction, which replaced the live action appearance of David Bowie with Raymond Briggs' very own Father Christmas voiced by Mel Smith. They also commissioned a documentary about The Snowman phenomenon, entitled *Snow Business* which features interviews with Raymond Briggs and the original animation team.

THE MERCHANDISE

Within a few years of his film debut, The Snowman was appearing on a wide range of products from stationery to textiles. In 1985 Royal Doulton secured the licence for interpreting his exploits in ceramic and before long these popular gifts became very collectable with prices snowballing on the secondary market for retired figures. Since 2000, the Coalport factory has had the UK licence to produce ceramic figures and giftware and their limited editions have been selling out within a few months.

Promotional Father Christmas plates and mug licensed by Blooming Productions.

A selection of The Snowman books.

The Snowman videos in a variety of languages.

Over the years, many other gift and collectable manufacturers have recognised the potential of The Snowman. There have been enamel boxes and other trinkets from Crummles and Border Fine Arts, artistic glass designs from Caithness Glass and Country Artists as well as decorations for the festive season from International Christmas. The Snowman has also been a phenomenal success in Japan with many products being commissioned exclusively by Sony Plaza. Snowman fans in Japan can find porcelain tableware, novelty glassware, water globes, musicals and miniatures. They can also win Snowman treasures by playing Sega machines in games arcades.

COPYRIGHTS

The licensing process for all Snowman products is strictly supervised by Copyrights, the merchandise agency run by Nicholas Durbridge and Linda Pooley. It is their job to ensure that the magic and innocence of The Snowman is not lost in the translation to other media. Licence agreements include detailed restrictions and requirements with close scrutiny and approval procedures for all prospective products at every stage of their development. When the finished piece finally goes into production, a royalty is payable based on a percentage of the price of the piece.

One of Copyrights' directors, Karen Addison, has worked with The Snowman character for twenty years, including her earlier career at

An illustration from *The Man* depicting a Royal Doulton Snowman mug.

Royal Doulton. During that time, she has been involved with hundreds of different products, including some surprising projects, such as a giant inflatable Snowman which is planned for production in time for Christmas 2004. Even after all these years, The Snowman film still has the power to move her and she is now enjoying the reaction of her own young children as they sit spellbound at the stage show. Given her attachment to this magical character, Karen is not surprised at the enduring quality of The Snowman, who celebrated his most successful Christmas ever in 2003.

THE DESIGNERS
Raymond Briggs has followed the development of his character with interest and has been impressed how well the licensees translated The Snowman into various media. It is not easy to transfer illustrations from the pages of a book to a three-dimensional image and the product designers need the ability to adapt, develop and change while remaining faithful to the quality of the story. It is a tribute to Royal Doulton's designers that Raymond Briggs included a drawing of one of their Snowman mugs in his later book, *The Man*, which was published in 1992.

WORLD-WIDE SUCCESS
The Snowman continues to be a best selling book, with 2.2 million copies sold in the UK to date and it has been translated into more than a dozen different languages, including Spanish, German, French, Italian, Norwegian, Icelandic, Taiwanese, Korean, Chinese, Japanese, Welsh, Dutch, Portuguese and Slovenian. The videos have also been released in many different countries, where The Snowman is known variously as Le Bonhomme de Neige, Sno Gubben, De Sneeuwman and Il Pupazzo di Neve.

ON STAGE
The versatile Snowman character stars in a stage show produced by the Birmingham Repertory Theatre, which has been performed every Christmas since 1998 in London's West End. In addition the theatre company has toured the production around the UK, as well as to Europe, Japan and the US and there is even a video of the show. More new characters have been created for the stage, such as the evil Jack Frost, and the sad ending of the story is softened by an encore of dancing Snowmen. The Snowman has also inspired a ballet, which was part of Scottish Ballet's repertoire for three years. In 1996, Hamleys, the London toy shop, chose animated scenes of The Snowman for their famous Christmas window decorations and he is a popular choice for Christmas grottoes all over the country.

THE SNOWMAN SELLS
The Snowman has been used to promote a diversity of companies and products, including an air conditioning system for Polo Volkswagen

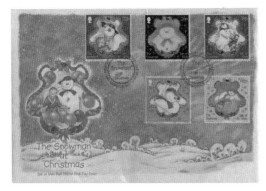

The Snowman 'First Day Cover' from the Isle of Man.

and a climate control system for Mitsubishi in Japan. TV adverts include an animation with a teddy for Toys R Us, which launched the Aled Jones record, and one for a Japanese version of chicken nuggets, which baffled Raymond Briggs as he could see no connection with the image of The Snowman. In Japan, The Snowman is also an incentive for fans to save at the Nishi-Nippon bank and play games at Sega's amusement arcades.

It was a proud moment when The Snowman was chosen to appear on a series of five stamps commissioned by Isle of Man post in 2003 and he was 'pleased and honoured' according to Raymond Briggs in the brochure which accompanied the first day cover. He must have been equally proud to star on the Isle of Man's fifty- pence coins and Raymond Briggs struck the first coin at Pobjoy Mint to launch the set. Gold, silver and cupro nickel diamond finish coins were produced in limited editions and the last two metals were also available in colour versions.

THE SNOWMAN CARES

Briggs has donated the services of The Snowman to charity on several occasions. He was one of the characters used to promote the BT National Swimathon in 1993. In the USA, artwork from the Snowman was featured in the 1998 mailing for the American Lung Association and reached 20 million American households. Also in 1998, Briggs allowed Childline to use The Snowman and Fungus the Bogeyman for their 'Back to School' anti-bullying campaign. Sales of The

Snowman badges raised over £75,000. Briggs also drew an exclusive Christmas card design for CLIC, the charity concerned with Cancer and Leukaemia in Childhood.

EXHIBITIONS

Framed prints and etchings have been made from The Snowman book illustrations by companies such as Manuscript and Sowa & Reiser and cels from the film have been reproduced by the key animators. To celebrate the twentieth anniversary of the film, Snowman Enterprises exhibited and sold some of the original drawings and production cels to collectors.

Original drawings by Raymond Briggs have been featured in several exhibitions, for example at the National Portrait Gallery in 2002 and the *Magic Pencil* at the British Library in 2003. At the 1998 *World of English Picture Books* Exhibition in Japan, The Snowman telephone cards and letter sets were sold as souvenirs. Raymond Briggs has achieved celebrity status in Japan and when he visited the country he was

The Snowman fifty-pence coins from the Isle of Man.

Raymond Briggs with The Snowman coins at the Pobjoy Mint.

The Snowman etchings by Sowa and Reiser.

The Snowman prints by Manuscript.

book. Perhaps it is the same students who are sometimes to be seen having their photographs taken beside the plaque outside the offices of Snowman Enterprises in London.

COLLECTORS

With this avalanche of merchandise, collectors all over the world are knee-deep in The Snowman products. Some focus on specific collections, such as the Royal Doulton and Coalport figures, others try to find every single piece of Snowman ephemera. Jerome and Rhonda Hanson in Seattle, set up new Snowman displays every Christmas, whilst in the UK Martin and Loraine Heywood enjoy The Snowman all year round in a special room of their house devoted to their collection. So dedicated are these particular collectors that they travelled all the way to Japan especially to look for Snowman memorabilia. Most collectors have to rely on the internet and e-bay to keep them in touch with the international world of The Snowman and knowledge of Japanese is a distinct advantage! There are several web sites with Snowman information that collectors can visit and details are given on page 99.

It seems that the enthusiasm for The Snowman in his many guises is destined to go on and on. Perhaps we should respond to Briggs' question 'Where will it all end?' in his own words. 'The Snowman doesn't know, he melted long ago. But his memory and image live on...'

astonished at his reception. One young Snowman fan was so overwhelmed to meet him that she broke down in tears. Each year, he is visited by a new group of Japanese children studying English literature and he takes them for a walk around the beautiful Sussex countryside, over which James and The Snowman fly in the

ROYAL DOULTON

Royal Doulton in Stoke-on-Trent was the first china company to recognise the potential of The Snowman for a collection of figures and giftware. Their marketing team was looking for new children's characters following the success of their Brambly Hedge and Beatrix Potter collections and after watching the video they realised that The Snowman was the perfect choice.

The Doulton company has a long tradition portraying characters from children's books. The first factory was established in London in 1815 and production of art pottery began at the Lambeth studio in the 1870s. Classics, such as *Alice's Adventures in Wonderland* and later *Wind in the Willows* provided some of the first artists with inspiration. The majority of Doulton figures, however, were made at their second factory in Burslem, Stoke-on-Trent, which was added to the company in 1877. By the 1920s, the Burslem artists were modelling popular cartoon characters, including Bonzo the dog, and Pip, Squeak and Wilfred from the *Daily Mail*. Interestingly, since childhood, Raymond Briggs has prized one of A.B. Payne's original drawings of Pip, Squeak and Wilfred, having asked for a sample of the cartoonist's work.

THE FIGURE COLLECTION

The John Beswick factory became part of the Royal Doulton group in 1969 and this brought more expertise in the production of popular children's characters. Design manager, Harry Sales, had worked with a succession of writers and illustrators to interpret their drawings for the ceramic process, notably Thelwell's shaggy ponies and Bestall's Rupert Bear. In 1984, Harry was given the task of translating the stocky, simplified shapes of The Snowman illustrations into three - dimensional figures. His solution was to introduce additional curves to the contours of the figures in order to create lively poses, which capture comical or enchanted moments from the tale. The figures were designed to interact with each other and so in the first group, launched in 1985, *James* DS1 can look up in wonder as his creation comes to life in *The Snowman* DS2 or he can admire his father's clothes on the *Stylish Snowman* DS3.

Harry Sales, designer of The Snowman figures.

Peter Roberts, designer of The Snowman giftware.

11

At first not everyone at Royal Doulton was convinced about The Snowman's sales potential – some argued he was too seasonal, others were concerned about the content of the predominantly white figures. Brand Manager,

Designs for The Snowman by Harry Sales.

Karen Addison, now a director of Copyrights, remembers the Arizona desert in temperatures of 40°C as the unlikely venue for a sales conference to launch Doulton's Snowman range internationally. The sceptics were soon proved wrong, however, and the initial collection of Snowman figures was so well received that Harry was soon working on a second collection. For this group, launched in 1986, he introduced some of the revellers from the snowmen's party, who appear in the animated film, including *Cowboy Snowman* DS6 and *Lady Snowman* DS8. These are now amongst the hardest Royal Doulton figures to locate as they were withdrawn before the others in 1992.

NURSERY AND GIFTWARE

Doulton's pattern designers also faced quite a challenge to recreate the soft crayon effect of Raymond Briggs' original drawings and to make a white snowman stand out against white bone china giftware. After much experimentation, Design Manager Peter Roberts came up with the idea of sketching directly on to the biscuit china. This is china before the translucent smooth white glaze is applied and the rough surface gave the granular crayon effect that he was searching for. The fact that prototype designs could be assessed on the actual china pieces proved to be an advantage as it gave an accurate insight into the look of the finished article. The choice of china shapes helped Peter Roberts to create an original effect as the embossed borders of the Gainsborough wall plates were left white to

Designs by Neil Faulkner for a party tray and plate which were not produced.

Prototype for a toast rack designed by Peter Roberts but not put into production.

resemble raised snow. A similar effect was achieved on the mugs and beakers by introducing a framed border that resembled a snowfall. By printing the snowflakes in raised white, he gave his designs an extra dimension and vibrancy on the blue sky background.

In the development of The Snowman giftware collection, Peter Roberts was assisted by Joanne Caine and Neil Faulkner, who also designed the packaging. Raymond Briggs followed their progress with enthusiasm, visiting the factory, approving the products and attending the launch at the National Exhibition Centre in 1985. He was very impressed with their work and commented, 'They really got into the spirit of the thing. Everything they have done is marvellous'.

NOVELTIES AND RARITIES

The ingenuity of the Doulton designers extended to novel giftware shapes, notably the 'Build a Snowman' breakfast sets, the Snowball money box and the Christmas tree ornaments, which were also assembled as a mobile. Some shapes, such as the salt and pepper set and the ginger jars, were only produced for a year and so they are very hard to find today.

Sadly not all The Snowman giftware designs came to fruition. Peter Roberts came up with the idea of a Snowman toast rack but it didn't go beyond the prototype stage and Neil Faulkner produced some wonderful plate concepts featuring The Snowman and James flying over the penguins, and a Snowman Christmas party, which were not approved for production.

From 1987 until 1990, the figure range was developed by the new Design Manager Graham Tongue and, together with modeller Warren Platt, he was responsible for the entertaining Snowman Band DS9-17 and the group of Snowmen playing in the snow DS20-23. Of these *The Snowman Skiing* DS21 remained in the range for less than two years and it now commands the highest price in the market place.

When Royal Doulton retired the entire collection of The Snowman figures and giftware in 1994, prices snowballed on the secondary market as collectors rushed to find all the pieces. However, the adventure began again in 1999 when Doulton Direct commissioned a limited edition collection of figures and tableaux to mark the twenty-first anniversary of The Snowman book. A relief modelled plaque of The Snowman and James 'Walking in the Air' was a novel addition to this late series which came to a poignant end in 2002 with *The Journey's End* tableau, depicting James with his melted Snowman.

FROM CONCEPT TO COLLECTOR'S CABINET

The journey from the original concept to the collector's cabinet is a long one and the creation of The Snowman figures involved many traditional crafts and skills at the John Beswick studios of Royal Doulton. When Harry Sales had completed his designs and they had been approved by Copyrights, they were given to David Lyttleton to create the first three-dimensional clay model. His finished figure had to be approved again by the licensor and any amendments made before it passed to the blockmaker who created the master mould. From the first block mould a number of prototype models were cast and a decorated piece prepared for approval. Once this had been passed for production, the various pieces of the figure were cast in working moulds using liquid clay. The figure was then assembled, dried and the seams removed before receiving its first firing. Each figure was then hand-painted before glazing and firing. One of the final touches was the application of the Royal Doulton backstamp.

ROYAL DOULTON FIGURES

DESIGNED BY HARRY SALES

DS1 James
Modeller   David Lyttleton
Height   3³/₄in (9.5cm)
Introduced 1985
Withdrawn   1993

DS2 The Snowman
Modeller   David Lyttleton
Height   5in (13cm)
Introduced 1985
Withdrawn   1994

DS3 Stylish Snowman
Modeller   David Lyttleton
Height   5in (13cm)
Introduced 1985
Withdrawn   1993

DS4 Thank You Snowman
Modeller   David Lyttleton
Height   5in (13cm)
Introduced 1985
Withdrawn   1994

DS5 Snowman Magic music box
This features the figure DS2
and plays 'Walking in the Air'
Height   8in (20.5cm)
Introduced 1985
Withdrawn   1994

DS6 Cowboy Snowman
Modeller   David Lyttleton
Height   5in (13cm)
Introduced 1986
Withdrawn   1992

DS7 Highland Snowman
Modeller   David Lyttleton
Height   5in (13cm)
Introduced 1986
Withdrawn   1993

DS8 Lady Snowman
Modeller   David Lyttleton
Height   5in (13cm)
Introduced 1986
Withdrawn   1992

DESIGNED BY GRAHAM TONGUE

DS9 Bass Drummer Snowman
Modeller   Warren Platt
Height   5¹/₂in (14cm)
Introduced 1987
Withdrawn   1993

DS10 Flautist Snowman
Modeller   Warren Platt
Height   5¹/₂in (14cm)
Introduced 1987
Withdrawn   1993

DS11 Violinist Snowman
Modeller   Warren Platt
Height   5¹/₄in (13.5cm)
Introduced 1987
Withdrawn   1994

DS12 Pianist Snowman
Modeller   Warren Platt
Height   5in (13cm)
Introduced 1987
Withdrawn   1994

DS13 Snowman's Piano
Modeller   Warren Platt
Height   5in (13cm)
Introduced 1987
Withdrawn   1994

DS14 Cymbal Player Snowman
Modeller   Warren Platt
Height   5¹/₄in (13.5cm)
Introduced 1988
Withdrawn   1993

DS15 Drummer Snowman
Modeller   Warren Platt
Height   5³/₄in (14.5cm)
Introduced 1988
Withdrawn   1994

DS16 Trumpet Player Snowman
Modeller   Warren Platt
Height   5in (13cm)
Introduced 1988
Withdrawn   1993

DS17 Cellist Snowman
Modeller   Warren Platt
Height   5¹/₄in (13.5cm)
Introduced 1988
Withdrawn   1994

DS18 Snowman music box
This features the figure DS7
and plays 'Blue Bells of Scotland'.
Height   8in (20.5cm)
Introduced 1988
Withdrawn   1990

DS19 The Snowman money box
Modeller   Graham Tongue
Height   8¹/₂in (21.5cm)
Introduced 1990
Withdrawn   1994

DS20 The Snowman Tobogganing
Modeller   Warren Platt
Height   5in (13cm)
Introduced 1990
Withdrawn   1994

DS21 The Snowman Skiing
Modeller   Warren Platt
Height   5in (13cm)
Introduced 1990
Withdrawn   1991

DS22 The Snowballing Snowman
Modeller   Warren Platt
Height   5in (13cm)
Introduced 1990
Withdrawn   1994

DS23 Building the Snowman
Modeller   Warren Platt
Height   4in (10cm)
Introduced 1990
Withdrawn   1994

DS2 The Snowman   DS1 James   DS3 Stylish Snowman

DS4 Thank You Snowman   DS5 Snowman Magic music box   DS6 Cowboy Snowman

DS8 Lady Snowman   DS18 Snowman music box   DS7 Highland Snowman

DS10 Flautist Snowman   DS9 Bass Drummer Snowman   DS11 Violinist Snowman

DS14 Cymbal Player Snowman   DS12 and DS13 Pianist Snowman and Piano

DS15 Drummer Snowman   DS16 Trumpet Player Snowman   DS17 Cellist Snowman

DS20 The Snowman Tobogganing   DS21 The Snowman Skiing   DS22 The Snowballing Snowman

DS19 The Snowman money box   DS23 Building The Snowman

DOULTON DIRECT

Dancing in the Snow tableau
To mark the 21st anniversary of
the book
Modeller   Shane Ridge
Height   5³/₄in (14.5cm)
Introduced 1999
Limited edition of 2,500

The Snowman and James (pair)
Modeller   Shane Ridge
Height   5³/₄ and 4¹/₂in
              (14.5 and 11cm)
Introduced 1999
Limited edition of 2,500

James Builds a Snowman (pair)
Modeller   Shane Ridge
Height   6ins and 4ins
              (15 and 10cm)
Introduced 2000
Limited edition of 2,500

The Adventure Begins tableau
Modeller   Shane Ridge
Height   6in (15cm)
Introduced 2000
Limited edition of 2,000

Walking in the Air plaque
Modeller   Shane Ridge
Height   8ins x 13in
              (20.5 by 33.5cm)
Introduced 2001
Limited edition of 2,500

Dressing the Snowman
Modeller   Shane Ridge
Height   6in (15cm)
Introduced 2002
Limited edition of 2,500

The Journey Ends tableau
Modeller   Shane Ridge
Height   4in (10cm)
Introduced 2002
Limited edition of 2,500

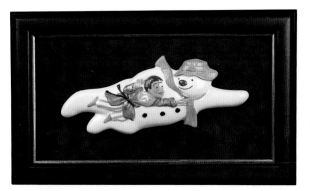

Walking in the Air plaque.

James Builds a Snowman (pair)   The Adventure Begins tableau

The Snowman and James (pair)   Dancing in the Snow tableau

Dressing The Snowman   The Journey Ends tableau

Dance of The Snowman   Snowman Christmas Cake   Walking in the Air

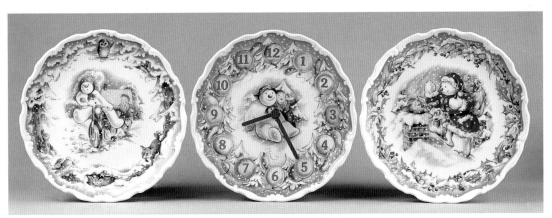

Snowman Rides a Motorbike   Snowman clock   Snowman's Visit.

WALL PLATES

Snowman Christmas Cake
Designer   Joanne Caine
Diameter   8¹/₂in (21.5cm)
Introduced 1985
Withdrawn 1994

Walking in the Air
Designer   Joanne Caine
Diameter   8¹/₂in (21.5cm)
Introduced 1985
Withdrawn 1994

Dance of The Snowman
Designer   Neil Faulkner
Diameter   8¹/₂in (21.5cm)
Introduced 1986
Withdrawn 1994

Snowman Rides a Motorbike
Designer   Neil Faulkner
Diameter   8¹/₂in (21.5cm)
Introduced 1987
Withdrawn 1991

Snowman's Visit
Designer   Neil Faulkner
Diameter   8¹/₂in (21.5cm)
Introduced 1990
Withdrawn 1994

Snowman clock
Designer   Neil Faulkner
Diameter   8¹/₂in (21.5cm)
Introduced 1989
Withdrawn 1994

Build The Snowman mug and soft toy.

BEAKERS

Walking in the Air (tall)
Designer   Joanne Caine
Height   4³/₄in (12cm)
Introduced   1985
Withdrawn   1994

The Party (tall)
Designer   Neil Faulkner
Height   4³/₄in (12cm)
Introduced   1985
Withdrawn   1994

The Snowman Band (low thin)
Designer   Joanne Caine
Height   3³/₄in (9.5cm)
Introduced   1988
Withdrawn   1994

Building The Snowman (low)
Designer   Joanne Caine
Height   3³/₄in (9.5cm)
Introduced   1985
Withdrawn   1994

Playful Snowman (low)
Designer   Joanne Caine
Height   3³/₄in (9.5cm)
Introduced   1985
Withdrawn   1994

Into the Forest (low)
Designer   Neil Faulkner
Height   3³/₄in (9.5cm)
Introduced   1989
Withdrawn   1994

Party Time set
Comprising tea plate, cup and saucer
Designer   Neil Faulkner
Diameter   6³/₄in (17.5cm)
Introduced   1986
Withdrawn   1994

Miniature tea set
Comprising plate, cup and saucer
Designer   Peter Roberts
Diameter   3³/₄in (9.5cm)
Introduced   1990
Withdrawn   1994

Children's set
Comprising plate, mug and cereal bowl
Designer   Peter Roberts
Diameter   8in (20.5cm)
Introduced   1989
Withdrawn   1994

Christmas Celebration set
Comprising baby plate, hug-a-mug and money ball
Designer   Peter Roberts
Diameter   6in (15cm)
Introduced   1991
Withdrawn   1994

Snowman money ball
Designer   Joanne Caine
Height   3¹/₂in (9cm)
Introduced   1985
Withdrawn   1994

Snowman savings book
Designer   Peter Roberts
Height   5in (13cm)
Introduced   1990
Withdrawn   1994

Balloons round box
Designer   Peter Roberts
Diameter   4in (10cm)
Introduced   1985
Withdrawn   1993

Highland Fling oval box
Designer   Joanne Caine
Diameter   3in (7.5cm)
Introduced   1985
Withdrawn   1993

Snowman Balloons coaster
Designer   Joanne Caine
Diameter   4³/₄in (12cm)
Introduced   1987
Withdrawn   1994

Build a Snowman set
Comprising an egg cup and dish
Designer   Peter Roberts
Height   4³/₄in (12cm)
Introduced   1985
Withdrawn   1992

Build a Snowman set
Comprising beaker, cereal bowl and plate
Designer   Peter Roberts
Height   5¹/₄in (13.5cm)
Introduced   1985
Withdrawn   1992

Ginger jar (large)
Designer   Peter Roberts and
    Joanne Caine
Height   6³/₄in (17.5cm)
Introduced   1990
Withdrawn   1991

Ginger jar (small)
Designer   Peter Roberts and
    Joanne Caine
Height   4in (10cm)
Introduced   1990
Withdrawn   1991

Salt and Pepper set
Designer   Peter Roberts
Height   3in (7.5cm)
Introduced   1990
Withdrawn   1991

Tree, Stocking, Snowman, James and Snowman Flying
Christmas tree ornaments
Designer   Peter Roberts and
    Joanne Caine
Height   3¹/₂in (9cm)
Introduced   1989
Withdrawn   1993

Snowman mobile
Designer   Peter Roberts and
    Joanne Caine
Height   3¹/₂in (9cm) each
Introduced   1985
Withdrawn   1993

Salt and Pepper set.

The Snowman Band; Walking in the Air; The Party; Building The Snowman; Into the Forest and Playful Snowman.

Balloons round box; coaster and Highland Fling oval box.

Party Time set and miniature tea set.

Children's set.

Christmas Celebration set.

Snowman money ball; savings book and Christmas Celebration money ball.

Build a Snowman sets, assembled.

Build a Snowman, two- and three-piece sets.

Ginger jars, large and small.

Snowman mobile.

Christmas tree ornaments.

Prototype music box which was not produced.

COALPORT

Designer Kevin Scully at work.

Coalport started the new Millennium with The Snowman licence and launched their first collection of china figures and giftware at the end of 2001. It was a runaway success with the first two limited editions selling out rapidly. Demand was so high that the six models in the general range had to be quickly re-ordered and the company reported sales of over 25,000 figures in the first three months. 2001 culminated in Coalport being awarded the 'Best Ceramic Gift Award' for The Snowman by the Guild of China and Glass Retailers. Coalport responded, 'We are overwhelmed by the success of The Snowman. It is the single most successful product launch in recent history'.

The Snowman has proved to be the perfect subject matter for this famous china company, which was established over 250 years ago on the banks of the River Severn in Shropshire. During the nineteenth century, Coalport displayed their ornamental china at the Great Exhibition and enjoyed the patronage of Queen Victoria. They also introduced their first figurative groups in

Parian ware, including a famous model of a cat and monkey in human dress. Figurine production was revived in the 1920s and continued after the company moved to Staffordshire in 1926 but the real renaissance of Coalport figures dates from the 1970s after the company became part of the Wedgwood group. A young team of modellers was invited to inject new life into their traditional range and classic characters, such as Little Grey Rabbit by Alison Uttley and Paddington Bear, the lovable bear from deepest Peru, became popular additions to the Coalport collection in the 1970s and 80s.

DESIGN AND MODELLING
When Coalport's marketing team was offered the chance to bid for The Snowman licence, they jumped at the chance as they felt this classic character was true to Coalport's traditional brand values. After watching the animated film several times, they came up with a list of memorable scenes that could be depicted in china. The ideas were then passed to Kevin Scully, a graphic

Design for The Band Plays On by Kevin Scully.

Design for a mug by Kevin Scully.

Design for an egg cup by Kevin Scully.

designer recommended by Copyrights, the licensing agency for The Snowman. Kevin is a Graphic Design graduate from Wimbledon School of Art, which coincidentally is where Raymond Briggs studied some twenty-five years earlier. Since the early 1980s, Kevin has worked as a designer and illustrator for many different sectors, including a storyboard artist for TV commercials. A few years ago, he was asked to produce some illustrations for Sainsbury's range of paper products featuring The Snowman and these were so well received that he has drawn The Snowman for Marks and Spencer, Volkswagen and Copyrights themselves. He has also been working on Raymond Briggs' other characters, Fungus the Bogeyman and Father Christmas.

For Coalport, Kevin Scully drew all the designs for the annual collectors' plates and the nurseryware collection. He also interpreted each scene from the film into a two-dimensional drawing showing front and back views to help the sculptor create the exact moment as a china figurine. Jenny Oliver was given the responsibility of modelling The Snowman figures and her interpretation is so good that she is now the only sculptor at Coalport authorised to work on the models.

THE FIGURE COLLECTION

For the Coalport Snowman collection, Jenny began with a figure of James *Building the Snowman* SM1 and then another of him *Adding a Smile* SM2. As the story unfolds through the figures, James watches his new friend dancing with his toys, stroking the cat, and experimenting with a new nose from the fruit bowl. At the end of the introductory collection, we are left in anticipation as James and The Snowman take off and *The Adventure Begins* SM5. In the second phase of the collection in 2002, the models become more complex as James and The Snowman enjoy the party at the North

Design for Walking in the Air by Kevin Scully.

Pole. For example, the limited edition tableau *The Band Plays On* SM14 incorporates three Snowman musicians with their instruments, including a piano with glasses of beer on top. Another special tableau, featuring James and The Snowman with Father Christmas, was introduced in 2003. This was the first time that Raymond Briggs' rather unconventional Father Christmas character had been included in The Snowman collection. *The Special Gift* SM32, as it is known, was offered first to members of the Coalport Collectors Club.

LIMITED EDITIONS

The Snowman limited editions have become so popular that several companies have commissioned exclusive models. The Guild of China and Glass Retailers has ordered several special figures, as has H. Samuel, the High Street jeweller and gift shop. UK International Ceramics, a company that made its reputation creating limited edition Bunnykins figures with Royal Doulton, has now discovered the appeal of The Snowman and has commissioned a series of figures and giftware from Coalport. *It's a Knockout Snowman* SM28 was the first of their exclusive figures to be launched in October 2003. Managing Director, Nick Tzimas, worked with graphic designer, Caroline Dadd, to visualise eight figures and a set of figural giftware, including a tea service, cookie jar, toothbrush holder and cotton wool dispenser for future production.

NOVELTIES

Coalport's Snowman collection already includes some innovative giftware items. The Snowman lithophane, introduced in 2003, revives an ancient ceramic art form, which uses the translucency of the china body to create pictures. Impressed designs are cast into the surface of the china and the beauty of the scene is revealed with a light source. Lithophane lamps were very fashionable in the nineteenth century and they were used as window hangings and fire screens in the twentieth century. The Snowman lithophane uses a tea light to illuminate the scene.

Another novelty item from Coalport is the advent calendar incorporating twenty-five little ceramic plaques, which young Snowman fans can turn over to reveal different scenes from the film. What a great way to anticipate Christmas and all the possible Snowman gifts, including a money box, book-end, a clock, glitter globes and Christmas decorations.

PRODUCTION AND SALES

When Coalport's marketing team began working on The Snowman collection, they considered long and hard where to make the pieces. They wished to price the figures competitively to appeal to all collectors, young and old, so they decided to source the figure collection from a modern, first class factory in Thailand, which uses bone china from a recipe supplied by a Stoke-on-Trent factory. The results have been exceptional with intricately detailed and finely painted models arriving promptly in the market place. In fact, the 2003 range went into the shops two months earlier than in previous years at the request of retailers and, once again, all the limited editions sold out even before they reached the shops because so many committed collectors pre-ordered.

The Coalport limited editions are now beginning to appear on e-bay at four or five times their original retail prices as collectors strive to create the complete set of figures. In this rapidly changing world of collectables, it's a good idea to keep up to date with new developments on the web, specifically at sites dedicated to The Snowman.

COALPORT FIGURES

The first production run of each new unlimited figure is marked 'FIRST EDITION'.

Designed by Kevin Scully
Modelled by Jenny Oliver

SM1 Building The Snowman
Height   3¼in (8cm)
Introduced 2001
Withdrawn 2002

SM2 Adding a Smile
Height   5½in (14cm)
Introduced 2001
Withdrawn 2003

SM3 Dancing with Teddy
Height   5½in (14cm)
Introduced 2001
Withdrawn 2003

SM4 The Wrong Nose
Height   5½in (14cm)
Introduced 2001
Withdrawn 2002

SM5 The Adventure Begins
Height   5in (13cm)
Introduced 2001
Withdrawn 2003

SM6 The Hug
Height   5¼in (13.5cm)
Introduced 2001
Withdrawn 2002

SM1 Building The Snowman   SM2 Adding a Smile   SM4 The Wrong Nose

SM3 Dancing with Teddy   SM7 Christmas Friends   SM5 The Adventure Begins

SM7 Christmas Friends
Height   5¾in (14.5cm)
Introduced 2001
Limited edition of 2,000

SM8 At the Party
Height   6in (15cm)
Introduced 2001
Limited edition of 2,000
Exclusive to the Guild of China
Retailers

SM9 The Greeting
Height   5¾in (14.5cm)
Introduced 2002 Current

SM10 Dressing Up
Height   5½in (14cm)
Introduced 2002 Current

SM11 Soft Landing
Height   4½in (11.5cm)
Introduced 2002 Current

SM12 Highland Fling
Height   5¼in (13.5cm)
Introduced 2002 Current

SM13 Hold on Tight
Height   6¾in (17cm)
Introduced 2002
Limited edition of 2,000

SM6 The Hug   SM8 At the Party   SM9 The Greeting

SM10 Dressing Up   SM11 Soft Landing   SM12 Highland Fling

SM15 The Merry Trio   SM14 The Band Plays On

SM17 Pulling a Cracker   SM13 Hold on Tight

SM18 Dancing at the Party   SM19 Hug for Mum   SM20 Snowman's Surprise

SM14 The Band Plays On
Height   6in (15cm)
Introduced   2002
Limited edition of 2,000

SM15 The Merry Trio
Height   5³/₄in (14.5cm)
Introduced   2002
Limited edition of 2,000
Exclusive to the Guild of China
Retailers

SM16 The Gift
Height   5¹/₄in (13.5cm)
Introduced   2002
Limited edition of 3,000
Exclusive to the Guild of China
Retailers

SM17 Pulling a Cracker
Height   5³/₄in (13.5 cm)
Introduced   2002
Limited to year of production
Exclusive to H. Samuel

SM18 Dancing at the Party
Height   4³/₄in (12cm)
Introduced   2003 Current

SM19 Hug for Mum
Height   5¹/₂in (14cm)
Introduced   2003
Withdrawn   2003

SM20 Snowman's Surprise
Height   5¹/₄in (13.5cm)
Introduced   2003
Withdrawn   2003

SM21 Cowboy Jig
Height   5¹/₄in (13.5cm)
Introduced   2003
Withdrawn   2003

SM22 Walking in the Air
Height   5¹/₄in (13.5cm)
Introduced   2003
Limited edition of 2,000

SM23 By the Fireside
Height   4¹/₂in (11.5cm)
Introduced   2003
Limited edition of 2,000

SM21 Cowboy Jig   SM22 Walking in the Air

SM16 The Gift

SM23 By the Fireside

SM24 Treading the Boards   SM25 Dance the Night Away   SM26 How do you do?

SM27 Sitting Pretty   SM28 It's a Knockout   SM29 Snowman with Friends

SM24 Treading the Boards
Height   5¹/₂in (14cm)
Introduced 2003
Limited edition of 2,000
Exclusive to the Guild of China
Retailers

SM25 Dance the Night Away
Height   4³/₄in (12cm)
Introduced 2003
Limited to the year of production
Exclusive to the Guild of China
Retailers

SM26 How do you do?
Height   5¹/₂in (14cm)
Introduced 2003
Limited to the year of production
Exclusive to H. Samuel

SM27 Sitting Pretty
Height   4³/₄in (12cm)
Introduced 2003
Limited to the year of production
Exclusive to H. Samuel

SM28 It's a Knockout
Height   5¹/₄in (13.5cm)
Introduced 2003
Limited edition of 1,000
Exclusive to UK International
Ceramics

SM29 Snowman with Friends
Height   5¹/₂in (14cm)
Introduced 2003
Limited edition of 1,000
Exclusive to UK International
Ceramics

SM30 Balancing Act   SM31 Play it Again   SM32 The Special Gift

SM33 Magical Moment

SM34 The Special Moment

SM30 Balancing Act
Height   6¹/₄in (16cm)
Introduced 2004
Limited edition of 1,000
Exclusive to UK International
Ceramics

SM31 Play it Again
Height   5³/₄in (14.5cm)
Introduced 2004
Limited edition of 1,000
Exclusive to UK International
Ceramics

SM32 The Special Gift
Height   5¹/₂in (14 cm)
Introduced 2003
Special gold backstamp in first
year of issue

SM33 Magical Moment
Height   5¹/₂in (14cm)
Introduced 2004 Current

SM34 The Special Moment
Height   5¹/₂in (14cm)
Introduced 2004 Current

SM35 The Bashful Blush
Height   5¹/₂in (14cm)
Introduced 2004 Current

SM35 The Bashful Blush

SM36 Hush! Don't Wake Them

SM37 All Together Now

SM45 The Welcome

SM46 Just Like Me

SM36 Hush! Don't Wake Them
Height   5¹/₂in (14cm)
Introduced 2004 Current

SM37 All Together Now
Height   5¹/₂in (14cm)
Introduced 2004
Limited edition of 2,500

SM38 A Cold Night In
Height   5¹/₂in (14cm)
Introduced 2004
Limited edition of 2,500
Not illustrated

SM45 The Welcome
Height   5¹/₄in (13.5cm)
Introduced 2004
Limited edition of 1,000
Exclusive to UK International
Ceramics at The Snowman Picnic

SM46 Just Like Me
Height   5¹/₄in (13.5cm)
Introduced 2004
Limited edition of 1,000
Exclusive to Coalport at The
Snowman Picnic

COALPORT NURSERY AND GIFTWARE

SMGW1
Mug
Height   3in (7.5cm)
Introduced   2002 Current

SMGW2
Plate
Diameter   7in (18cm)
Introduced   2002 Current

SMGW3
Bowl
Diameter   6in (15cm)
Introduced   2002 Current

SMGW4
Divided dish
Length   8³/₄in (22.5cm)
Introduced   2002 Current

SMGW5
Egg cup and soldiers tray
Length   9¹/₄in (23.5cm)
Introduced   2002 Current

SMGW6
Three piece set
Plate, mug and bowl
Diameter   7in (18cm)
Introduced   2002 Current

SMGW7
Advent calendar
With 25 ceramic plaques on a
wooden stand
Height   9in (23cm)
Introduced   2002 Current

SMGW8 The Snowman
Money box
Height   7in (18cm)
Introduced   2002 Current

SMGW9
Mug – large (two images)
Height   4in (10cm)
Introduced   2002 Current

SMGW10
Mug – large (five images)
Height   4in (10cm)
Introduced   2002 Current

**SMGW11 James and The
Snowman Hugging**
2003 annual plate
Diameter   8in (20.5cm)
Introduced   2002

SMGW12
James, Snowman, Cake, Tree
Christmas tree decorations
(set of four)
Height   3in (7.5cm)
Introduced   2002
Exclusive to H. Samuel and
Wedgwood shops

SMGW8 The Snowman money box.

SMGW10 large mug, SMGW2 plate, SMGW1 mug, SMGW3 bowl, SMGW4 divided dish, SMGW5 egg cup
and soldiers tray, SMG9 large mug.

SMGW7 Advent calendar.

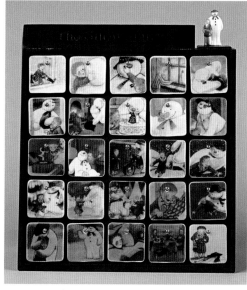

SMGW7 The reverse of the advent calendar plaques.

SMGW17 Dancing at the North Pole.

SMGW11 James and The Snowman Hugging.

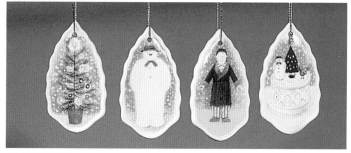

SMGW12 Christmas tree decorations.

SMGW13 Christmas Friends
Glitter globe
Height   5½in (14cm)
Introduced 2002 only

SMGW14 The Snowman and James
Book-end
Height   5½in (14cm)
Introduced 2003 Current

SMGW15 The Snowman and James
Clock
Height   5in (13cm)
Introduced 2003 Current

SMGW16
Lithophane
Height   2½in (6.5cm)
Introduced 2003 Current

SMGW17 Dancing at the North Pole
2004 annual plate
Diameter   8in (20.5cm)
Introduced 2003

SMGW18 Hold on Tight
Glitter globe
Height   5¼in (13.5cm)
Introduced 2003 only

SMGW19 Treading the Boards
Glitter globe
Height   5¼in (13.5cm)
Introduced 2003
Limited edition of 2,000
Exclusive to the Guild of
China Retailers

SMGW20 Walking in the Air
Glitter globe
Height   5¼in (13.5cm)
Introduced 2004 Current

SMGW15 The Snowman and James clock.

SMGW14 The Snowman and James book-end.

SMGW24 The Snowman and Lady Snowman salt and pepper set.

SMGW16 Lithophane.

SMGW13 Christmas Friends   SMGW18 Hold on Tight   SMGW19 Treading the Boards

SMGW20 Walking in the Air   SMGW21 The Hug

SMGW21 The Hug
Glitter globe
Height   4½in (11.5cm)
Introduced   2004
Exclusive to Collectors Choice

SMGW23 Treading the Boards
2005 annual plate
Diameter   8in (20.5cm)
Introduced   2005

**SMGW24 The Snowman
and Lady Snowman**
Salt and pepper set
Height   3¾in (8cm)
Introduced   2004
Limited edition of 1,000
Exclusive to UK International
Ceramics.

COMPTON AND WOODHOUSE

Walking in the Air
Plate
Diameter   8in (20.5cm)
Introduced   2002
Limited edition of 9,500
This Coalport plate was
commissioned by Compton
and Woodhouse and test
marketed by direct mail.

Compton and Woodhouse plate.

SMGW23 Treading the Boards,
design for annual plate, 2005.

ENAMELS
CRUMMLES AND BORDER FINE ARTS

The Snowman has been featured on a variety of enamel boxes by Crummles and Border Fine Arts as well as other collectable trinkets, such as thimbles and bells. Enamel boxes were very fashionable in Georgian England and were given as love tokens or souvenirs to be used for all manner of personal effects from patches to snuff. The English became the acknowledged experts in the art of enamelling on copper following the invention of transfer printing in the mid-eighteenth century but this specialist craft virtually died out in the wake of the industrial revolution. After considerable research, the technique was revived in 1970 and enamel boxes once again became popular gifts and collectables.

CRUMMLES

To cater for this new interest, Crummles and Company was founded in 1974 and, along with traditional designs, they produced enamel boxes featuring characters from children's stories. The Tales of Beatrix Potter provided the inspiration for the first collection in 1978 and this was followed by other classics, including Paddington Bear, Winnie the Pooh and Brambly Hedge. The licence to reproduce The Snowman characters was granted in 1985 and Crummles introduced a collection of six round and oval boxes in various sizes. Later, between 1999 and 2001, Crummles produced a series of limited edition Snowman boxes especially for Doulton Direct, a mail order company for china and collectables.

Since 2001, Crummles has been part of the Staffordshire Enamels group in the heart of the Potteries but The Snowman boxes were produced at their original workshops in Poole, Dorset using manufacturing processes that have changed very little since the 18th century. First of all, the box is shaped from a thin sheet of pure copper and layers of enamel are fired on repeatedly until a fine glazed finish is perfected. Next, the outline transfer is applied to the enamel and fired into the surface. The artists then paint the boxes by hand using specially mixed enamel colours which are applied and fired many times to achieve a rich, glowing effect. Finally, the bezel and hinge are made from brass, silver soldered and hand-finished.

Crummles for Doulton Direct:

| The Snowman Greeting | Meeting The Snowman | Dancing with The Snowman |
| The Snowman and James | Walking in the Air | James Builds The Snowman |

Meeting The Snowman
The Snowman Dancing

The Snowman Flying
The Snowman Hugging James

Building The Snowman
The Snowman Greeting

CRUMMLES ENAMELS

XR1429 The Snowman Dancing
Small round box
Diameter   1^1/4in (3.5cm)
Introduced 1985
Withdrawn 1995

XR1430 The Snowman Greeting
Small round box
Diameter   1^1/4in (3.5cm)
Introduced 1985
Withdrawn 1995

MR1425 Meeting The Snowman
Medium round box
Diameter   1^1/2in (4cm)
Introduced 1985
Withdrawn 1995

Building The Snowman
Medium round box
Diameter   1^1/2in (4cm)
Introduced 1985
Withdrawn 1995

VR1427 The Snowman Hugging James
Oval box
Diameter   2in (5cm)
Introduced 1985
Withdrawn 1995

LPRY 1424 The Snowman Flying
Large round box
Diameter   2^1/2in (6cm)
Introduced 1985
Limited edition of 500

CRUMMLES FOR DOULTON DIRECT
Walking in the Air '1999'
Large round box
Diameter   2^1/2in (6cm)
Introduced 1999
Limited edition of 1,978 to mark the publication of the book in 1978.

The Snowman and James '2000'
Large round box
Diameter   2^1/2in (6cm)
Introduced 2000
Limited edition of 1,978 to mark the publication of the book in 1978.

James Builds The Snowman
Large round box
Diameter   2^1/2in (6cm)
Introduced 2001
Limited edition of 500

Meeting The Snowman
Dancing with The Snowman
The Snowman Greeting
Set of three boxes
Diameter   1^3/4ins and 1^1/4in
                (4.5cm and 3 cm)
Introduced 2001
Limited edition of 500

BORDER FINE ARTS

Border Fine Arts has only recently entered the enamels market, having built its reputation with realistic resin sculptures of wildlife and farming scenes. The company was founded in 1974 by John Hammond and from its humble beginnings around a kitchen table in the picturesque Scottish Borders, it grew rapidly into a highly successful company. In 1989, Border Fine Arts began to distribute products for the Enesco Corporation of Illinois, USA, one of the world's leading producers of fine gifts, collectables and decorative accessories. The successful partnership between the American and Scottish companies was cemented in 1995 when Enesco bought Border Fine Arts. Since the merger, Border Fine Arts has diversified into different media, including pottery and enamels, and has sought out many successful licensed properties.

Over the years, Border Fine Arts has created figurines inspired by the Tales of Beatrix Potter, Jill Barklem's Brambly Hedge and Flower Fairies, so they fully appreciated the qualities of classic characters like The Snowman. Working with Copyrights, they developed a range of enamel boxes depicting scenes from the book and added inscriptions underneath the lids. Border Fine Arts also revived the eighteenth-century concept of toys, which were small versions of familiar household objects, created for the amusement of adults. Ladies of leisure would delight in arranging their little treasures in display cabinets or dolls' houses, for these were not then the preserve of the young. The Border Fine Arts collection of enamels includes a little teapot, cup and saucer, a trinket tray, a covered box, a clock, a bell, a thimble and a photo frame.

The magic of The Snowman artwork combined with this traditional art form, will ensure that enamel boxes and other little treasures will delight contemporary collectors as much as their Georgian ancestors.

BORDER FINE ARTS ENAMELS

A3995 The Snowman and James Dancing
Large trinket tray
Diameter   6in (15cm)
Introduced   2003 Current

A3996 The Snowman and James Flying
Rectangular box
Height   1¼in (3cm)
Introduced   2003 Current

A3997 The Snowman Portrait
Round box
Height   1¼in (3cm)
Introduced   2003 Current

A4001 The Snowman with Balloons
Oval box
Height   1½in (3.5cm)
Introduced   2003 Current

A4002 The Snowman and James
Clock
Height   4¾in (12cm)
Introduced   2003 Current

A4003 The Snowman
Photo frame
Height   4½in (11.5cm)
Introduced   2003 Current

A4004 The Snowman and James Flying
Cup and saucer
Height   2½in (6.5cm)
Introduced   2003 Current

A4006 The Snowman and James Dancing
Teapot
Height   4in (10cm)
Introduced   2003 Current

A4007 The Snowman and James Dancing
Covered box
Height   4½in (11.5cm)
Introduced   2003 Current

A4008 The Snowman and James Dancing
Bell
Height   3¾in (9.5cm)
Introduced   2003 Current

A4010 The Snowman
Thimble
Height   1¼in (3cm)
Introduced   2003 Current

A4011 The Snowman
Square box
Height   1½in (3.5cm)
Introduced   2003 Current

BORDER FINE ARTS ENAMELS

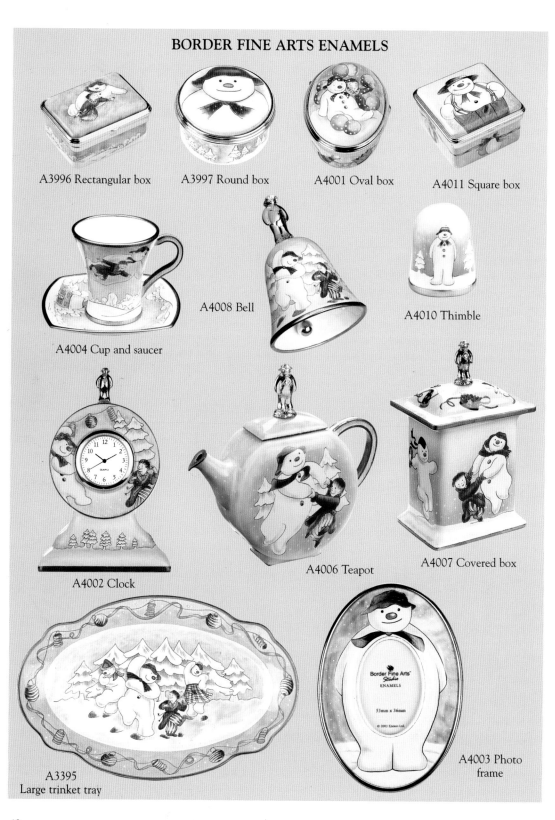

A3996 Rectangular box

A3997 Round box

A4001 Oval box

A4011 Square box

A4004 Cup and saucer

A4008 Bell

A4010 Thimble

A4002 Clock

A4006 Teapot

A4007 Covered box

A3395
Large trinket tray

A4003 Photo
frame

ART GLASS
CAITHNESS GLASS AND COUNTRY ARTISTS

CAITHNESS GLASS

The icy, reflective qualities of art glass make it an excellent medium for portraying the exploits of The Snowman and the Scottish company, Caithness Glass, explored the magical effects of snow and light for their famous paperweights collection.

Caithness Glass was established in the far north east of Scotland in 1961 to produce contemporary hand-blown glass in the Scandinavian tradition. Within a few years, the company was best known for their paperweights and created an entirely new look for this art form with their enigmatic abstract designs. Over the years, Caithness Glass paperweights have been made in myriad shapes, sizes and colours, the modern ones with imaginative swirls, twirls and bubbles and the traditional in millefiori patterns or lampwork scenes. Glass paperweights are extremely tactile objects and each paperweight constantly changes depending on the angle from which it is viewed.

For a few years in the late 1990s, Caithness Glass was part of the Royal Doulton group and this led to a commission for four limited edition paperweights depicting The Snowman for sale through Doulton Direct, the mail order division of the company. The scenes on the paperweights were delicately engraved into the glass, which is facetted to create intriguing effects of magnification and reflections. The deep blue colour of the glass resembles a night sky, whilst the tiny bubbles suggest starry snowflakes and the exuberance of James and The Snowman's adventure. Walking in the Air was the first scene to be introduced in 2000 and this evocative image was also engraved on a stunning art vase which Caithness introduced in 2002.

There are different methods of engraving on glass and Caithness Glass uses traditional copperwheel techniques or a sandblasting process to create various depths in the glass. A

revolutionary new technique using laser technology to create internal fractures in glass is now being used by Country Artists to create their Crystal Treasures collection featuring The Snowman.

A Caithness Glass paperweight being made.

Detail of Caithness Glass paperweight, The Adventure Begins.

CAITHNESS GLASS

These pieces were made exclusively for Royal Doulton and distributed by Doulton Direct

Walking in the Air
Paperweight
Diameter   3in (7.5cm)
Introduced 2000
Limited edition of 750

Dancing in the Snow
Paperweight
Diameter   3in (7.5cm)
Introduced 2001
Limited edition of 750

The Adventure Begins
Paperweight
Diameter   3in (7.5cm)
Introduced 2001
Limited edition of 750

Thank You Snowman
Paperweight
Diameter   3in (7.5cm)
Introduced 2001
Limited edition of 750

Walking in the Air
Vase
Height   8in (20cm)
Introduced 2002
Limited edition of 500

Caithness Glass vase, Walking in the Air.

Caithness Glass paperweights: Thank You Snowman; Walking in the Air and Dancing in the Snow.

COUNTRY ARTISTS

Country Artists, situated in the Warwickshire Countryside, has been in business since 1978. Traditionally a resin based figurine company, they have branched out over the years into other types of giftware. Having secured the licence to use images from The Snowman, they launched a new collection of three-dimensional crystallised sculptures in 2003. The Crystal Treasures designs are based on artwork from the animated film and the cels are used by their team of artists to produce computer generated mock-ups. These are then submitted to a computer modeller who uses software modelling tools to create a virtual 3D model. This is a highly skilled and time consuming process and the modeller must be very artistic as well as computer literate to capture the charm of The Snowman imagery and translate two-dimensional images into three-dimensional models.

Once the final image has been approved, it can then be fired into the crystal blocks using the latest laser technology which causes a minute internal fracture. The blocks may contain as many as 200,000 fractures, the density of which affects the translucency of the image. Only the finest quality optical crystal is used and skilled craftsmen hand-finish each block by polishing and bevelling the glass to enhance the lead crystal's natural refractive and reflective qualities. So impressed were the Guild of Specialist Gift Retailers with this new art form that they immediately ordered an exclusive limited edition piece *Over Brighton Pier* and a key-ring featuring *The Greeting*.

COUNTRY ARTISTS

56400 The Snowman
Height   3¹/₄in (8cm)
Introduced 2003 Current

56401 The Meeting
Height   2¹/₂in (6cm)
Introduced 2003 Current

56402 Walking in the Air
Height   2¹/₂in (6cm)
Introduced 2003 Current

56403 Dancing in the Snow
Height   2¹/₂in (6cm)
Introduced 2003 Current

56404 Flying over the Pier
Height   2¹/₂in (6cm)
Introduced 2003 Current

56405 The Farewell
Height   2¹/₂in (6cm)
Introduced 2003 Current

56406 The Greeting
Key-ring
Height   1¹/₂in (4 cm)
Introduced 2003 Current
Exclusive to the Guild of Specialist Gift Retailers

56407 Over Brighton Pier
Height   2¹/₂in (6cm)
Introduced 2003
Limited edition of 1,000
Exclusive to the Guild of Specialist Gift Retailers

56406 The Greeting key-ring   56407 Over Brighton Pier

56400 The Snowman   56401 The Meeting   56402 Walking in the Air

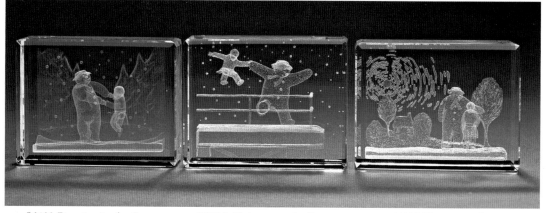

56403 Dancing in the Snow   56404 Flying over the Pier   56405 The Farewell

SNOWMAN ENTERPRISES

The Snowman
'20 years on film'
Engraved glass coaster
Introduced 2003
Limited edition of 25 for VIP distribution.
Commissioned by Snowman Enterprises

Snowman Enterprises glass coaster.

WATER GLOBES, MUSICALS AND OTHER NOVELTIES

WATER GLOBES

Watching a miniature fantasy world encased in glass is an endless source of fascination and this accounts for the timeless appeal of water globes. These are hollow globes filled with water and when shaken, a flurry of snowflakes or starry crystals fills the sky and slowly settles on the scene below. Water globes come in many different styles and qualities, from glass spheres incorporating miniature china models on polished wooden bases, as produced by Coalport (see page 38), to cheap and cheerful plastic examples which are ideal Christmas stocking fillers. One of Raymond Briggs' favourite pieces was a limited edition resin water globe made in 1999 as a promotional piece for Borders Books in the USA by Westland Giftware. Sega Enterprises, who run games arcades in Japan, commissioned a set of five colourful resin water globes for their popular crane games (see page 90). Often the water globes have musical mechanisms in the base and most Snowman models play the haunting theme tune 'Walking in the Air'.

MUSICALS

Musicals featuring The Snowman have been made for the US and Japanese markets where they are particularly collectable (see also page 70). Silvestri, the Christmas specialist in the US, commissioned an entertaining resin model of The Snowman and James attached to a wire so that they can 'Walk in the Air' in time to the music. They also produced a magnetic musical in which The Snowman glides across the ice as the music plays, plus a range of little Snowman figures as Christmas tree ornaments.

PVC

PVC figures of film and TV characters have a collector following, especially in the USA where there are clubs to support this enthusiasm. Often these little figures are given away with fast food meals and boxes of cereal or purchased for modest sums at souvenir shops. One of the leading manufactures of PVC figures is Bully of West Germany, suppliers to Disney and other distributors of desirable characters such the Smurfs, My Little Pony and TinTin. They secured a licence for The Snowman in 1989 and made a range of PVC figures, some of which were also featured in water globes and attached to key-rings, magnets, clips and pen holders.

NOVELTIES

Promotional products which are given away are often difficult for collectors to find as they are not necessarily valued by the original recipients. For example the novelty plant pots produced for a promotion at Tesco food shops in 1998 are pretty elusive today.

Similarly badges, buttons and pins featuring The Snowman are hard to find because of their ephemeral nature. In the 1980s, Royal Doulton gave away Snowman badges to promote their product range and Elgin Court attached badges to their Christmas cards. The Childline charity campaign raised £75,000 with the sale of rubber Snowman badges made by The Big Badge Company. Fans can also look out for the set of enamel pins, featuring The Snowman in different guises, and a blinking badge made in Japan.

Several companies have sought The Snowman licence for decorating clocks. In the UK, Royal Doulton and Coalport have both included china clocks in their Snowman collections and Cloverleaf, better known for their place mats and mugs, made a melamine wall clock especially for Marks and Spencer in 1988. In addition Housemartin, which later became Spearmark International, produced wall mounted, pendulum and alarm clocks in different materials. Sony Plaza also licensed clocks for their stores and for the Sega Games machines (see page 90).

Silvestri resin, Chinese plastic and Westland resin water globes.

412010 International Christmas water ornament.

41205 International Christmas musical.

WESTLAND GIFTWARE USA

Resin water globe with/without snow
Height   5¹/₄in (13.5cm)
Introduced   1999
Limited edition of 9,000
This water globe was produced as a promotional piece for Borders Books and made in China

INTERNATIONAL CHRISTMAS

412010 The Snowman 'Snow Storm'
Water ornament
Height   3¹/₂in (9cm)
Introduced   2003 Current

41205   Walking in the Air
Musical
Height   13¹/₄in (33cm)
Introduced   2003 Current

412028   The Snowman with James
Set of two resin figures
Height   10¹/₄in (26cm)
Introduced   2004 Current

412029   The Snowman with James
Set of four resin figures
Height   5³/₄in (14.5cm)
Introduced   2003 Current

SILVESTRI USA

Walking in the Air
Resin music box
Height   6¹/₂in (16.5cm)
Introduced   c.1988
Made in China

The Snowman Party
Resin musical water globe
Height   5¹/₂in (14cm)
Introduced   1991
Made in Taiwan

The Snowman and James
Plastic water globe
Height   3¹/₂in (9cm)
Introduced   1991
Made in China

The Snowman with Animals
Resin music box
Height   6¹/₂in (16.5cm)
Introduced   1991
Made in China

The Snowman Ice Skating
Magnetic music box
Height   4in (10cm)
Introduced   1991
Made in Taiwan

The Snowmen Dancing
Plastic music box
Height   4in (11.5cm)
Introduced   1991
Made in China

Christmas tree decorations (10)
Height   2³/₄in (7cm)
Introduced   1991

INTERNATIONAL CHRISTMAS RESIN FIGURES

412028A The Snowman with James Dancing.

412028B The Snowman with James.

412029 The Snowman with James.

Silvestri Snowmen Dancing music box.

Silvestri Snowmen Christmas tree decorations.

Silvestri Snowman Ice Skating, Snowman with Animals and Walking in the Air music boxes.

KEITH BUTTERS UK
Snowman and James with Balloons
Snowman and James in the Forest
Porcelain novelty plant pots
Height   3in (7.5cm)
Introduced 1998
Withdrawn 2000
Made for a Tesco promotion

CLOCKS

HOUSE MARTIN UK
Later Spearmark International
Wall clocks, alarm clocks and
pendulum clocks

Alarm clock
Height   7in (18cm)
Introduced 1986
Made in West Germany

Pendulum clock
Height   12in (30.5cm)
Introduced 1986
Made in Britain

Cloverleaf
Melamine wall clock for Marks and
Spencer
Introduced 1988
3,000 of these clocks were produced
Not illustrated

PVC FIGURES AND NOVELTIES

BULLY, WEST GERMANY
PVC figures hand-painted in West
Germany
**Snowman and James Dancing
'I Love You'**
**Snowman with Teddy 'Ach, Das
Leben Kann Sooo Schon Sein'**
**Snowman with Present 'Frohe
Festtage'**
Pen holders
Height   3in (7.5cm)
Introduced 1989

Snowman and James Dancing
Pen holder
Height   4in (10cm)
Introduced 1989

Keith Butters plant pots made for Tesco.

House Martin pendulum and alarm clocks with Star clock for Sony Plaza, Japan.

PVC and plastic jewellery by Bully and other makers.

Snowman with Heart
'Thank you' – blue
Snowman and James Hugging
'Danke' – red
Snowman with Teddy
'Danke' – red
Snowman with Teddy
'Thank you'
Snowman with Balloons
'Herzlichen Gluckwunsch'
Heart boxes
Height   4in (10cm)
Introduced 1989

Snowman with Teddy
Snowman with Present
Highlighter pens
Height   3in (7.5cm)
Introduced 1989

Snowman and James Hugging
Paperclip
Height   3¹/₂in (9cm)

Snowman and James Dancing
'Love'
Snowman and James Hugging
'Love'
Heart clip
Height   3¹/₂in (9cm)
Introduced 1989

Snowman with Balloons – red
Snowman with Heart – white
Pencil sharpener
Height   3¹/₂in (9cm)
Introduced 1989

Snowman with Heart
Snowman with Balloons
Magnet
Height   2¹/₂in (6.5cm)
Introduced 1989

Snowman and James Hugging
Snowman and James Dancing
Suction ornaments
Height   2¹/₂in (6.5cm)
Introduced 1989

Snowman and James Dancing
Snowman with Balloons
Plastic clips
Height   3ins (7.5cm)
Introduced 1989

Snowman with Teddy
Snowman and James Dancing
Snowman with Heart
Key-rings
Height   2¹/₂in (6.5cm)
Introduced 1989

Snowman with Balloons in
Armchair
Pink and blue
Height   4in (10cm)
Introduced 1989

Snowman Dancing
Ear-rings, brooch, bracelet and
hair clips
Height   1¹/₂in (4.5cm)
Introduced 1989

The Snowman
Brooches
Height   2¹/₂in (6cm)
Introduced 1989
This jewellery was packaged by
Jane Designs

All of the above characters are
found as free-standing PVC figures.
Similar figures have also been
found in lead.

BADGES

ROYAL DOULTON
'The Snowman will melt your
heart'
Button badge
Diameter   2¹/₂in (6.5cm)
Introduced 1985

Bully PVC figures and other novelties.

Lead Snowman figures in the same styles as Bully PVC.

'Happy Christmas from the Snowman'
Button badge
Diameter   2¹/₂in (6.5cm)
Introduced 1986

Button badges for Elgin cards
Diameter   2¹/₄in (6cm)
Introduced 1988

DAIWA INTERNATIONAL CO LTD, JAPAN
'The Pin that Blinks'
Introduced   1995 and 1999
Not illustrated.

THE BIG BADGE COMPANY
Snowman Pin
Height   1¹/₄in (3cm)
Introduced   1999
Made for Childline's 'Back to School' anti-bullying campaign

Snowman Dancing
Snowman Flying
Snowman and James Sledging
Snowman Dressing Up
Enamel badges
Height   1¹/₄in (3cm)
Introduced   1995

ABBEYCREST
Gold and Silver Snowman charms
Height   ³/₄in (2cm)
Introduced   1989
Test only not produced

Big badge Snowman pin, enamel badges and Royal Doulton promotional badge.

Abbeycrest gold and silver charms, not produced.

Happy Christmas badge 1986.

Elgin Court cards with badges.

THE SNOWMAN CHRISTMAS

GREETINGS CARDS

The Snowman has become part of our Christmas culture ever since the film was first screened in December 1982 – as traditional as mince pies and Santa Claus. He has become a favourite for Christmas card designs and several different manufacturers have sought licences to feature The Snowman on greetings cards, gift tags and wrapping paper. In the UK, Elgin Court was the first to see his potential in 1984, followed by Obpacher Verlag in Europe and Paper House Productions in the USA, producers of die-cut Snowman shaped cards. Marks and Spencer have chosen The Snowman for their own range of Christmas cards on more than one occasion and over the years they have commissioned Snowman advent calendars, a Christmas stocking, party cakes, and decorative tins full of chocolates for the festive season.

GIFT TINS

Colourful tin boxes, packaged with biscuits or sweets, are popular gifts at Christmas time and are usually saved long after their contents are eaten. In fact, so useful are decorative tins for storage that they are often sold empty in nests of varying sizes. Today's ephemera is often tomorrow's collectable so perhaps the various Snowman tins will become very sought after in the future. Amongst the companies which have produced Snowman tins are Kinnerton Confectionery, Jacobsen's Bakery, the Barnsley Canister Company and Hotcakes, who produced a novelty tin in the form of a Christmas cracker. Real Snowman Christmas crackers have also been produced with Snowman souvenirs inside.

TOILETRIES AND TOYS

Attractively packaged toiletries are desirable Christmas gifts and in the UK Grosvenor of London used to present Snowman shaped soaps and foam bath in seasonal gift boxes. They also made fluffy Snowman coat hangers, packaged in pairs for Christmas. Cuddly Snowman toys in lots of different sizes are often found under the Christmas tree. Originally these were made by Golden Bear and then Eden Toys but since 2001 Snowman soft toys have been produced by the Prestige Toy Corporation, which also offers baby's rattles in the form of The Snowman and melamine tableware for baby's first meals. In 2003, Steiff, the most prestigious teddy bear manufacturer, introduced a limited edition Snowman in a memorable scene from the film 'Dancing with Teddy', which was sold exclusively by the Guild of Specialist Gift Retailers.

GAMES

The Snowman has inspired his own board game, made originally by Pic Toys, and he has starred on countless jigsaws, magnetic play sets, card games and dress-up play sets. For creative children, there are art sets, paint by numbers, stencil sets and sewing kits whilst for youngsters who prefer electronic pastimes, there are interactive CD roms, Sony Playstation games and mobile phone games.

The Snowman from Royal Doulton at Christmas time.

CHRISTMAS DECORATIONS

The Snowman is ideally suited as an ornament for the Christmas tree and these have ranged from bone china pendants made by Royal Doulton and Coalport to cute resin tree trims from International Christmas. This enterprising company has ensured that The Snowman is part of today's Christmas experience with a range of resin ornaments, gift bags, a fibre optic Snowman light and an animated figure of The Snowman playing 'Walking in the Air' on the violin.

The Snowman can help decorate the Christmas table with place mats and coasters and there have been several ranges of disposable partyware over the years. A number of companies have produced Snowman candles to create a festive atmosphere on the table and the Christmas cake. Even the cake itself can be in the shape of The Snowman, thanks to the Tesco confectionery ranges for 2003 and 2004.

With all these seasonal offerings, Raymond Briggs has become a bit like his own Father Christmas character. As he struggles to unpack boxes and boxes of Snowman samples, he jokingly complains of 'another blooming Christmas' with the Snowman and is amused at the irony of being most famous for books set around the festive season.

Colour version of the fifty-pence coin from the Isle of Man.

CHRISTMAS CARDS

ELGIN COURT
Various designs
Christmas cards
(Including cards with badges
Plus exclusive designs for W.H.
Smith)
Gift wrap and tags
Introduced 1984-1991

GEMMA INTERNATIONAL
Greetings cards
Gift wrap and tags
Party invitations
Thank you notes
Introduced 2000-2005

BOOTS
Made by International Greetings
Christmas cards boxed
Gift wrap and tags
Christmas crackers
Introduced 1997-1998

PAPER HOUSE PRODUCTIONS
Woodstock, NY, USA
Various die-cut designs
Introduced 1998

A selection of Christmas cards.

MARKS AND SPENCER
Made by Hallmark Cards –
Tigerprint Division
Gift wrap and tags
Bags
Advent calendar
Christmas cards
(Including special family designs)
Introduced   1998-2003

PETER RABBIT AND
FRIENDS
Christmas card
Gift wrap and cards
Hat/scarf and mittens set
Introduced   1999-2003

OBPACHER VERLAG
Christmas Cards
(Frohe Weihnachten und ein
Gluckliches Neues Jahr
Frohe Festtage und ein Gutes Neues
Jahr)
Book of sixteen postcards
(De Sneeuwman & De Kerstman)
Introduced   1988-1992

CALTIME
Advent calendars
Christmas card holders
Introduced   1995

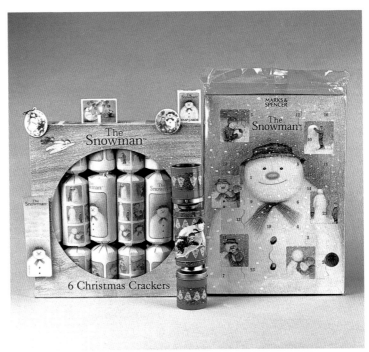

Marks and Spencer's advent calendar, crackers and Hotcakes tin cracker.

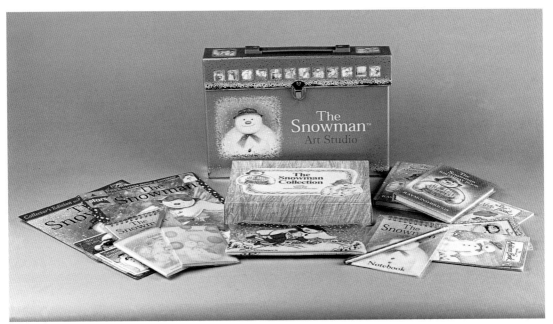

Snowman magazines, Copywrite, Claremont and Sony stationery and Robert Frederick art set.

Grosvenor toiletries and coat-hangers, Wisdom toothbrushes with Japanese toothbrush sets and mirrors.

STATIONERY

COPYWRITE STATIONERY
Paper based products, including notebooks, sketch and writing pads, jotters, pencils, sharpener, eraser, coloured pencils and party paperware
Introduced 1985-1988

PAPER HOUSE PRODUCTIONS USA
Note-cards, stickers, photo cards
Introduced 2001

ROBERT FREDERICK
Art sets
Puzzle cubes
Photo albums
Gift wrap, tags and bags
Gift boxes
Advent calendars
Introduced 2000 Current

Notebook
Address book
Place mat set
Introduced 2003 Current

TOILETRIES

GROSVENOR OF LONDON
Foam bath and picture soap set
Foam bath, soap and liquid soap set
Snowman coat-hangers
Introduced 1988-1991

ADDIS
Wisdom toothbrushes

GOULDS
Tissues
Toilet tissue
Kitchen towels
Introduced 2000-2003

JAMONT
Kitchen towels
Introduced 1994

TIN GIFT BOXES

SCHWEDT & GESING
Small tins in various shapes and sizes
Introduced 1994

INTERGOODS BAKERY, DENMARK
Changed to Jacobsen's bakery
Variety of tins for
Chocolate Chip Cookies
Introduced 1990-2004

KINNERTON CONFECTIONERY
Variety of tins for sweets and chocolates
Chocolate tree decorations
Advent calendar
Shaped figures
Introduced 1988-2003

MARKS AND SPENCER
Variety of tins for sweets and biscuits
Introduced 1991

ELITE GIFTS
Changed to Hotcakes
Snowman cracker tin unfilled
Introduced 2002-2004

BARNSLEY CANISTER COMPANY
for Ravenmere Marketing
Variety of tins
Introduced 1986

Tin wares by BSB, Icarus, Barnsley Canister and Marcel Schurman.

Kinnerton, Marks and Spencer and Intergoods Bakery tins for biscuits and sweets.

BSB
Tin boxes, tray, nests of tins
Cardboard nests of boxes
Introduced 1989

MARCEL SCHURMAN
Tin box and cardboard boxes
Cardboard boxes – nest of three
Introduced 1990

ICARUS (TOYS AND GAMES)
Tin waste bin and play tray
Plastic place mats
Introduced 1988-1991

JIGSAWS AND TOYS

HESTAIR HOPE
Jigsaw puzzles
Introduced 1985-1988

EARLY LEARNING CENTRE
Jigsaw – 48 pieces
Introduced 1992

PIC TOYS
Board game
Lacing kits
Stencil kits
Painting by numbers
Introduced 1988-1991

SUSAN PRESCOT GAMES
Lotto
Card domino
Board game
Jigsaws
Introduced 2000-2003

BSB
Mini jigsaw
Matches
Introduced 1989

KIDSTAMPS USA
Rubber stamps
Introduced 1995-1999

GOLDEN BEAR PRODUCTS
Soft toys
Mobiles
Musical toys
Wash mitt and soap (for
Mothercare)
Introduced 1985-1991

Jigsaws from UK and Japanese manufacturers.

EDEN TOYS
Soft toys – various sizes
Puppets
Nursery mobiles
Flock figures
Soft slippers
Melamine gift set
Magnetic play set
'Make Your Own' playset
1988-2000

PRESTIGE TOY CORPORATION
Distributed in the UK by Rainbow Designs
Soft toys – various sizes
Beanbag toys
Musical pull toys
Soft rattles
Jack in the Box
Melamine gift set
Magnetic play set
Dress up play set
Security blanket toys
Introduced 2001 current

STEIFF
Snowman with teddy
Exclusive to the Guild of China and Glass Retailers
Introduced 2003
Limited edition of 1,500

Steiff Snowman with teddy.

International Christmas animated Snowman with violin.

Soft toys from Eden Toys.

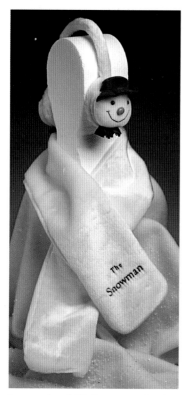

International Christmas scarf and ear muff set.

Candlepower candles, BSB matches, Lakeland cake decorations and Azuma lamp.

CRAFTS

WILLIAM BRIGGS
Long-stitch kits
Introduced 1989

ROBIN WOOLS
Knitting kits
Introduced 1991

INTARSIA
Knitting pattern booklet
Introduced 1992

SIRDAR
Instructions for knitted sweaters
and toys
Introduced 2000-2003

RAGGED ROBIN DESIGNS
Cross-stitch kits
Introduced 2000-2001

MURDOCH BOOKS
Books of counted cross-stitch charts
Introduced 2000-2003

SUPERCAST
Plaster and candle moulding sets
Introduced 1991-1996

CLOTHES AND ACCESSORIES

FRANKEL AND ROTH
Canvas satchel and tote bag
Introduced 1985

SHREDS
Adult PVC apron
Children's tabard
Adult and children's bags
(Including designs for Hamleys)
Purse
Pencil case
Introduced 1985-2003

INTERNATIONAL CHRISTMAS
Snowman scarf and ear muff set
Slippers
Introduced 2003

CANDLEPOWER
Snowman shaped candles
Christmas cake candles
Introduced 1985-1988

BEAR, BEAR AND BEAR
Cake decorating candles
Introduced 1996-2000

SALISBURY GIFT COMPANY
Candles
Introduced 2003

CANDLES AND CHRISTMAS ORNAMENTS

INTERNATIONAL CHRISTMAS
Fibre Optic Sitting Snowman
Animated Snowman playing the violin
Resin Snowman tree trim
Snowman place mats and coasters
Paper carrier bags
Introduced   2003

ATLAS LACE PAPER
Party paperware
Introduced   1988-1989

UNIQUE IMAGES
Party paperware
Christmas crackers
Introduced   2000-2002

FINE ART DEVELOPMENT
Christmas crackers
Introduced   1991

DELGADO
Christmas crackers for Toys R Us
Introduced   1995

Salisbury candles.

International Christmas fibre optic Snowman with Star.

International Christmas resin tree trim.

SONY PLAZA

The Snowman has experienced phenomenal popularity in Japan, mainly thanks to Sony Plaza, the licence holders and sub agents who have promoted a vast range of character merchandise. Sony Plaza is a member of the Sony group, which incorporates a variety of businesses along with their innovative electronic products. Sony Plaza was established in 1966 to introduce a variety of first class products manufactured outside Japan to the Japanese public. It is a unique company because it is a combined importer, wholesaler and direct retailer. They have their own stores all over Japan as well as franchise outlets and this has enabled them to be extremely successful in developing a market for high-quality merchandise of good design. Paddington Bear, Elmer the Patchwork Elephant, and The Snowman are amongst the classic characters that they have promoted to their customers all over Japan.

In the late 1980s, Sony Plaza imported Royal Doulton's Snowman collection, which they featured in their lavishly illustrated Snowman catalogue along with decorated Japanese glassware and ceramic music boxes known as orgels. There was also an abundance of The Snowman soft toys, clothes, slippers, towels, toiletries, lunch boxes, sweets and cookies, jigsaw puzzles, stationery and books.

GLASS
The Japanese glassware seems to have been very popular as different Snowman designs were applied each year. There were four main styles of drinking glasses, including one in the shape of James' wellington boot, which was made in two sizes. Initially the glass was plain with colourful enamelled motifs but frosted glass was introduced in the 1990s as well as a bright blue tumbler with white snowflake designs. Votive candleholders were made in decorated and sculptured glass and Sony Plaza also offered figurative candleholders of The Snowman in ceramic, one showing him flying with a candle on his back and the other with a candle in his hat.

ORGELS
Many of the Japanese ceramic figures of The Snowman have a musical mechanism in the base to make them into orgels. The Japanese are fascinated with musicals and there are several museums dedicated to the history of mechanical musical movements, including one which boasts the earliest recorded example from 1796. There are twelve orgels illustrated in Sony Plaza's 1989 catalogue, ranging from two to five inches, and some of the smaller designs are presented under a dome. Four new designs were made by Sekiguchi in the mid 1990s together with a figurative Snowman photo frame. Larger music boxes were made in a matt finish ceramic body by Tsukamoto, another Japanese company. A feature of these 1992 designs is the flying Snowman and James model, which extends on a wire above the scene and revolves when the music plays.

CHINA
When Royal Doulton retired their range of Snowman nursery and giftware in 1994, Sony Plaza looked for a new manufacturer and their 1995 catalogue features a selection of plates, mugs, teacups and saucers made in Korea. This seems to have been a short lived venture, however, and the majority of the Japanese porcelain tableware was made by the Azuma Company from 1997 until 2002. An extensive Azuma collection of coffee cups, mugs, teapots, canisters, plates, bowls and spoons was licensed by Sony Plaza for distribution through the Kiddyland company outlets in Japan, Singapore, Taiwan and Hong Kong. Azuma also made miniature doll's house furniture and tea sets in porcelain as well as little bells and candleholders. Electric lights and glass ornaments for light fittings or window hangings completed the range. On the expiry of Azuma's licence, Yamaka Shoten, a well known Japanese ceramic housewares manufacturer introduced a collection of china for Christmas 2003, which included mugs, plates, cookie jars, tea for one set and bottle stoppers.

THE SNOWMAN IS EVERYWHERE

In addition to all the china and glass products, which are now being sought after by collectors, Sony Plaza also distributed a wide range of Snowman goods in other media, including PVC, plastics, textiles and paper. Since the late 1980s, Japanese children have been able to fill their day with The Snowman in a variety of guises. When The Snowman alarm clock goes off in the morning, they could dress in Snowman T-shirts, socks, hats and aprons, accessorised with brooches. They could carry meals to school in plastic lunch-boxes with matching cutlery in a tote bag or rucksack. Their stationery, writing materials and cases could all feature The Snowman as well as their key-ring, which could even be musical. In the evenings, they could watch the Snowman video and play with jigsaw puzzles in a room furnished with cushions, mats and soft toys. For dinner they could have chicken nuggets promoted by The Snowman on TV and as a special treat they could have Snowman cookies or sweets, served with a drink in a Snowman tumbler. At bedtime, they could put on their Snowman pyjamas and slippers, wash and brush their teeth with various toiletries and towels and go to sleep with their Snowman night-light.

Japanese adults could also surround themselves with Snowman products in the home, including enamel cooking pots and pans, fridge magnets, thermal flasks and mugs, storage tins and serving trays, lamps and candles. Appropriately there are Snowman ice-cream makers, ice crushers and electric fans for cooling off but perhaps the strangest manifestation of The Snowman is on a range of bathroom accessories including a toilet brush holder and dust box. No wonder two keen collectors in the UK booked a trip to Japan just to go Snowman shopping!

SEGA AND TAITO

One of the most entertaining ways to collect The Snowman in Japan is to head for the amusement arcades and try to grab one of the prizes in the crane game machine. Between 1998 and 2002, Sega Enterprises held a licence from Sony Plaza to produce a variety of Snowman novelties for their arcade machines in Japan. The Sega

Japanese Crane game machine with Utsumi Sangyo pans.

Corporation, which was founded in 1951, is well known for its portable electronic games, but it is also the world leader in coin-operated arcade games. They had several uses for The Snowman imagery, including Print Club frames for stickers and screen images for mobile phones.

Amongst the treasures to grab in the Sega arcade crane games were china mugs and clocks, frosted glass tumblers and plates, water globes, plastic wind-chimes and revolving lanterns, towels in a tin, and silver metal charms. Most of the Sega gifts were sourced from manufacturers in Asia and produced in huge quantities, for example around 18,000 water globes were made.

Snowman premiums can also be won in the arcade machines of another Japanese company, Taito Corporation. Lucky players can go home with Snowman ceramics, a stuffed toy, a cushion, a Christmas wreath or a plastic globe light with snowflake designs.

In Japan, premium products are given away when purchasing certain products or spending a certain amount of money. Customers expect free gifts at car dealers, petrol stations and even when renewing newspaper delivery subscriptions. Utsumi Sangyo specialises in manufacturing and distributing premium and giveaway products for commercial use and they held a Snowman licence in 2003. Amongst the products they produced were ceramic mugs, plates and cutlery sets, a thermos flask, a clock, a lamp and candles.

NISHI-NIPPON BANK

To encourage young Japanese women to save money, Snowman incentives were offered by the Nishi-Nippon bank in Fukuoka. Established in 1944, Nishi-Nippon is one of Japan's most prominent financial institutions and it is a measure of The Snowman's popularity in Japan that they chose him as their image character. Depending on how much money they deposited, savers could look forward to a variety of customer bonuses, such as vanity cases, tissue holders, umbrellas, sports towels, clocks, glasses and a range of china. The china shapes included a mug, a teapot, a jar and plates decorated with different images of The Snowman and James. The Snowman has also appeared on the bank's stationery and there are savings books, cash cards and cheque holders printed with different Snowman designs all under licence from Sony Plaza.

The International Bank of Taipei in Taiwan also offered Snowman incentives to clients who made purchases of a certain amount on their credit cards. This promotion was licensed by Copyrights Asia and included amongst the gifts were Snowman soft toys, picture books and videos.

SONY PLAZA GLASS

Snowman Dancing
Snowman Standing
Boot glass – clear
Height   5¹/₄in (13.5cm)
Introduced 1989

Snowman and Penguin
Boot glass – clear
Height   5¹/₄in (13.5cm)
Introduced 1990

James Hugging Snowman
Snowman and James Sledging
Boot glass – clear mini set of two
Height   4in (10cm)
Introduced 1991

Snowman and James with Present
Boot glass – clear set of two
Height   5¹/₄in (13.5cm)
Introduced 1992

Snowman Dancing
Snowman Drinking
Snowman Playing Flute
Snowman Playing Accordion
Boot glass – clear mini set of four
Height   3in (7.5cm)
Introduced 1992

James with Snowmen
Boot glass – frosted
Height   5¹/₄in (13.5cm)
Introduced 1993

Snowman in a variety of poses
Boot glass – clear mini set of two
Height   4in (10cm)
Introduced 1993
Not illustrated

Snowman Flying
Boot glass – frosted
Height   5¹/₄in (13.5cm)
Introduced 1994

Snowman Flying (red and blue)
Boot glass – frosted mini set of two
Height   4in (10cm)
Introduced 1994

Snowman in a variety of poses
Boot glass – frosted mini set of two
Height   4in (10cm)
Introduced 1994

Frosted boot glasses in two sizes.

Clear boot glasses in three sizes.

Clear mini boot glasses.

Designs for boot glasses.

Clear tumblers.

Snowman in Snow
Snowman in a variety of poses
Glass tumbler – clear with foot
Height   4in (10cm)
Introduced 1989

Snowman Standing
Snowman Party
Glass tumbler – clear straight
Height   4¹/₄in (11cm)
Introduced 1989

Snowman Dancing
Snowman Running
Glass tumbler – tall clear flute
Height   6¹/₄in (16cm)
Introduced 1989

James Greeting Snowman
James Dancing at Snowman Party
James and Snowman with Cake
Glass tumbler – clear with foot
Height   4in (10cm)
Introduced 1990

Snowman and James Sledging
Snowman and James Landing
Glass tumbler – clear straight
Height   4¹/₂in (11cm)
Introduced 1990

Designs for tumblers.

Clear tumblers.

Frosted candleholders, tumbler and paperweight.

Snowman Playing Accordion
Snowman and James with
Balloons
Glass tumbler – tall clear flute
Height   6in (15cm)
Introduced 1990

Snowman and James with Teddy
Glass tumbler – frosted straight
Height   3¹/₄in (8.5cm)
Introduced 1992

James Greeting Snowman
Snowman in a variety of poses
Glass tumbler – clear straight
Height   5in (13cm)
Introduced 1993

Snowman Standing
Snowman and James on
Motorbike
Glass tumbler, clear straight set of two
Height   4¹/₂in (11.5cm)
Introduced 1993

MISCELLANEOUS

Paperweight – frosted
Diameter   3¹/₂in (9cm)
Introduced 1988

Snowman Dancing
Glass candleholder – frosted
Height   2¹/₄in (5.5cm)
Introduced 1992

Glass votive
Relief decoration
Height   2³/₄in (7cm)
Introduced 1992

Snowman and Snowflakes
Blue glass
Height   4¹/₂in (11.5cm)
Introduced 1994

Blue glass tumbler.

SONY PLAZA ORGELS AND OTHER NOVELTIES

Tsukamoto music boxes.

Sekiguchi orgels.

TSUKAMOTO
Flying with Penguins
Music box
Height   9in (23cm)
Introduced 1992

Flying over House
Music box
Height   9in (23cm)
Introduced 1992

Snowman and James Dancing
Music box
Height   4³/₄in (12cm)
Introduced 1992

Snowman and James Dancing
with Lady Snowman
Music box
Height   4in (10cm)
Introduced 1992

SEKIGUCHI
Made in Japan

Meeting Snowman
Hugging Snowman
Dancing with Snowman
Playing with Balloons
Orgel
Height   5¹/₄in (13.5cm)
Introduced 1989

Sekiguchi catalogue page of orgels.

Tsukamoto design for music box.

Snowman with Teddy
Lady Snowman
Orgel
Height   6³/₄in (17.5cm)
Introduced 1989

Snowman Standing
Snowman on Roller Skate
Snowman Waving
Orgel
Height   4¹/₄in (11cm)
Introduced 1989

Lady Snowman
Snowman Dancing
Snowman and James
Orgel with dome
Height   4in (10cm)
Introduced 1989

Snowman and James Sledging
Orgel
Height   4in (10cm)
Introduced 1994

Candleholders and Snowman with Penguin figure.

Snowman with Teddy seated
Orgel
Height   4in (10cm)
Introduced 1994

Snowman with Balloons
Orgel
Height   4in (10cm)
Introduced 1994

Snowman Dancing with Teddy
Orgel
Height   4½in (11.5cm)
Introduced 1994

Snowman and Teddy
Musical photo frame
Height   3½in (9cm)
Introduced 1995

Snowman with Hat
Candleholder
Height   4in (10cm)
Introduced 1994

Snowman Flying
Candleholder
Length   5in (12.5 cm)
Introduced 1994

Snowman with Penguin
Figure
Height   4in (10cm)
Introduced 1994

Design for glass holder.

CERAMIC GIFTS

Snowman
Glass holder
Introduced 1992

Snowman
Toothbrush holder
Introduced 1992

Snowman
Photo frame
Introduced 1992

Snowman and James Sledging
Photo frame
Height   5¼in (13.5cm)
Introduced 1992
Not illustrated

Design for toothbrush holder.

Design for photo frame.

Bathroom clocks for the Nishi-Nippon Bank.

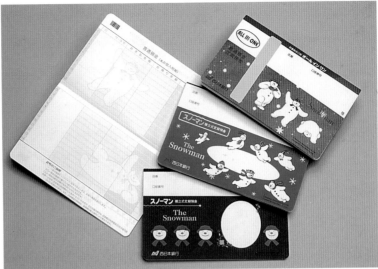

Savings books for the Nishi-Nippon Bank.

NISHI-NIPPON BANK
Savings books – five designs
Introduced 1996
Also cheque holders

Snowman with Penguin
Plate
Diameter   6³/₄in (17cm)
Introduced 1996

Snowman and James with Cake
Plate
Diameter   6³/₄in (17cm)
Introduced 1996

Plastic vanity case
Length   3¹/₄in (8cm)
Introduced 1996

Mug
Height   3³/₄in (9.5cm)
Introduced 1996

Glass
Height   6in (15cm)
Introduced 1997

Alarm clock
Height   4in (10cm)
Introduced 1997

China, glass and plastic incentives for the Nishi-Nippon Bank.

Large cup
Height   2¹/₂in (6cm)
Introduced 1997

Jar
Height   4³/₄in (12cm)
Introduced 1997

Teapot
Height   4³/₄in (12cm)
Introduced 1997

Tissue holder
Height   4³/₄in (12cm)
Introduced 1998

Bathroom clock
Pink and blue
Height   5¹/₂in (14cm)
Introduced 1997

Also umbrellas, sports towels, calendars and screen savers

SONY PLAZA NURSERY AND TABLEWARE

Plates, mugs, teacups and saucers made in Korea.

Designs for tableware made in Korea.

Porcelain tableware
Inscribed 'Follow the story of a little boy called James who builds a Snowman. That night his Snowman comes alive and takes James on a magical journey.'
Made in Korea

James Running and Hugging Snowman
James Meeting Snowman
Flying with Snowman
Riding Motorbike
Mug
Height   4in (10cm)
Introduced 1995

Cup and saucer
Height   2¹/₂in (6cm)
Introduced 1995

James Hugging Snowman
James and Snowman Flying
Plate
Diameter   7¹/₄in (18.5cm)
Introduced 1995

Snowman Portrait heads
Snowman Party
Mug
Introduced 1995

Cup and saucer
Introduced 1995

ARAI MOUNTAIN AND SKI RESORT
Snowman with Skis
Mug
Height   3¹/₄in (8cm)
Introduced 1994

Arai Mountain and Ski Resort mug.

Azuma teapot, canister, mugs, spoons, teacup and saucer.

Azuma bowls and teapot stand.

AZUMA COMPANY

The backstamp reads 'Snowman Enterprises Ltd 1997 Licensed by Sony Plaza Co. Ltd. Used under licence by Azuma Co. Ltd.

James and Snowman Dancing James and Snowman with Balloons
Tableware
Introduced 1997
Withdrawn 1999

85104/204
Mug
Height   3¹/₄in (8.5cm)

85121/221
Coffee cup and saucer
Height   2³/₄in (7cm)

85129/229
Mug with lid and strainer
Height   4in (10cm)

85117
Herb teapot
Height   4¹/₂in (11cm)

85127
Teapot stand
Diameter   6in (15cm)

85122
Small cake plate with floral border
Diameter   6¹/₄in (16cm)

85123
Cake plate
Diameter   7³/₄in (19.5cm)

85124
Party plate
Diameter   10¹/₄in (26cm)

85125
Curry and spaghetti bowl
Diameter   6¹/₂in (16.5cm)

85126
Oatmeal breakfast bowl
Diameter   6¹/₂in (16.5cm)

85128
Multi use bowl
Diameter   4¹/₂in (11cm)

85130
Small condiment bowl
Diameter   4in (10cm)

85131/231
Canister
Height   5³/₄in (14.5cm)

85101-501
Coffee spoon – six designs
Length   5¹/₄in (13.5cm)

85180/280
Photo frame
Height   6³/₄in (17.5cm)

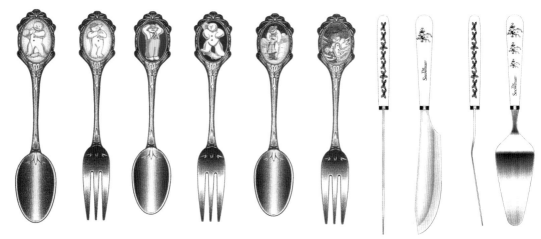

Designs for Azuma spoons, forks and serving sets.

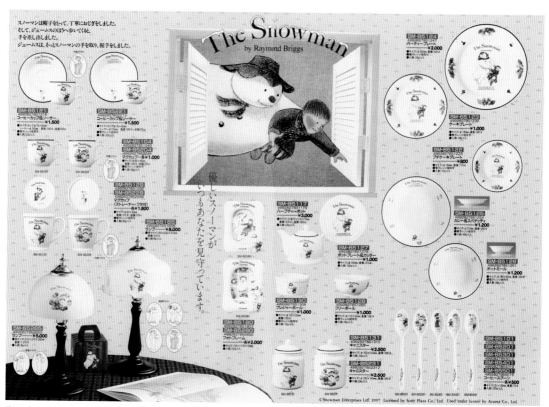

Catalogue page of Azuma tableware and lamps.

Azuma cup.

Designs for Azuma cups and mugs

Designs for Azuma plates.

Designs for Azuma plates and pots.

MINIATURE PORCELAIN SETS

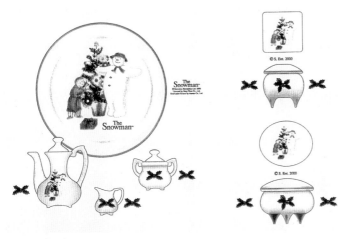

Designs for Azuma miniatures.

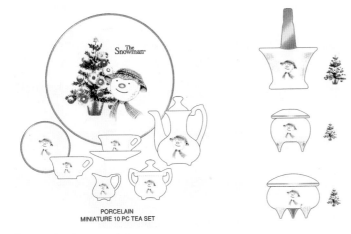

PORCELAIN
MINIATURE 10 PC TEA SET

Designs for Azuma miniatures.

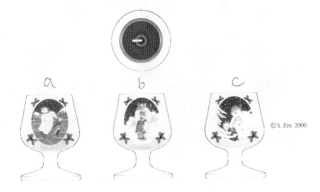

Designs for Azuma candle holders.

Snowman and James with Christmas tree
Introduced 2000
Miniature coffee set – four pieces
Comprising plate, coffee pot, sugar and cream

Miniature cup and saucer – two pieces

Miniature plate – two pieces

Miniature plate – three pieces

Miniature furniture – four pieces
Comprising sofa, table and two chairs

Miniature furniture – six pieces
Comprising chest, table and four chairs

Miniature furniture – three pieces
Comprising sofa and piano with seat

Miniature cup with candle – pair

Miniature cup and round box with candles and bell

Miniature boxes with candles, round, oval and square – three pieces

Snowman's Head
Miniature tea set – ten pieces

Miniature furniture set – seven pieces

Miniature flower vases – six shapes
Basket
Submitted 2000

Snowman and James Dancing in Snowflakes
Big plate
Big pot for three or four
Mini pot for one
Introduced 1999

Snowman and James Flying over Penguins
Snowman and James with Christmas Tree
Snowman head with Christmas Tree
Snowman and James in Forest
Snowman and James Hugging
Snowman and James Skating
Cups, mugs and plates and mini candle cups
Introduced 2000

Azuma miniature furniture.

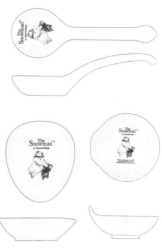

Azuma ceramic spoon and rest

CUTLERY

James and Snowman Dancing
Ceramic spoon and rest
Submitted   1999

Snowman Boxing
Snowman Skateboarding
Snowman with Hot Water Bottle
Snowman and James in Forest
Snowman and James Hugging
Snowman Dressing Up
Metal spoon and fork set with
ceramic disc
Submitted   1999

Snowman Head and Christmas Tree
Cake and salad serving sets with
ceramic handles
Submitted   2000

AZUMA GLASS AND LAMPS
Glass window ornaments
Introduced   2000

Snowman and James Hugging
Oval portrait
Height   5¼in (13.5cm)

Snowman and James Flying over Penguins
Oval landscape
Height   5in (13cm)

Snowman and James in Forest
Round
Height   4½in (11cm)
This design was also available with
an electric light

Snowman and James Dancing
Oval with light fitting
Height   4¾in (12cm)

85265
Electric lamp – glass shade with
wooden stand
Height   13in (33.5cm)
Introduced   1997
See illustration on page 62.

Snowman and James Flying
Electric lamp
Height   14¼in (36cm)
Introduced   2000

Designs for Azuma glass ornaments.

YAMAKA-SHOTEN

The Snowman (blue border)
The Snowman (white border)
Snowman and James Hugging
Porcelain tableware
Inscribed on reverse: 'The Snowman.
The night the Snowman came alive
and took James on a magical journey.'
Plate
Diameter   7³/₄in (20cm)

Mug
Height   4ins (10cm)

Cup and saucer
Height   2¹/₂in (6cm)
Introduced 2003

Cake plate and tea plates with inscriptions.

Snowman and James Flying
Snowman and James Taking Off
Snowman and James Hugging
Snowman and James Shaking Hands
Snowman Dressing Up
Inscription on plates: 'The Snowman
adopts himself to the life of James and
spends an enjoyable time.'

Cake plate
Diameter   9¹/₂in (24cm)

Tea plate
Diameter   6³/₄in (17cm)

Bowl
Diameter   6¹/₄in (17cm)
Not illustrated

Cup without handle
Height   3¹/₂in (9cm)

Cups and spoons with inscriptions.

Teacup and saucer with blue border.

Teacup and saucer with blue border.

Plates and mugs with blue border.

Cup with handle
Height 3in (7.5cm)
Not illustrated

Japanese teacup without handle
Height 3in (7.5cm)
Not illustrated

Mug with strainer and lid
Also sold without lid
Height 3³/₄in (9.5 cm)
Not illustrated

Child's mug
Height 3in (7.5cm)
Not illustrated

Divided dish
Length 10³/₄in (27.5cm)
Not illustrated

**Snowman and James Dancing
Snowman Head**
Mug and Towel sets
Height 3¹/₂in (9cm)
Introduced 2003

Figurative nurseryware
Snowman shaped plate
Length 10¹/₄in (26cm)
Introduced 2003

Snowman head cup with hat lid
Height 3¹/₂in (9cm)

Snowman spoon holder
Height 5¹/₂ins (14cm)

Spoon
Length 4¹/₂in (11.5cm)

Snowman head cup
with hat lid.

Snowman shaped plate.

Mug and plate
with white border.

Teacup and
saucer with white border.

Snowman spoon holder.

Pink mug and towel set.

Blue mug and towel set.

Snowman with stars mug.

Patchwork mug.

Yellow and red stripes mug.

Snowman and Stars
Mugs in red, blue and green
Height   3¹/₂in (9cm)

Patchwork
Red and blue bands
Yellow and red stripes
Mugs
Height   3³/₄in (9.5cm)

UTSUMI SANGYO LTD
Premiums and incentives
Ceramic plate, mug, cake plate,
cutlery, glass pot
Introduced 2003

Yamaka-Shoten tableware display in a Japanese store.

Utsumi Sangyo plate.

Utsumi Sangyo mug.

NOVELTIES

Snowman with Penguin
PVC money box
Height   7¼in (18.5cm)
Introduced   1994
Made in China

'Touchpon' light
Made in China
Height   7¾in (19.5cm)
Introduced   2000

Snowman Standing
Snowman Taking Off
Snowman Flying
Fridge magnets
Height   3¼in (8cm)
Introduced   1994

Snowman Dancing
Snowman with Present
Snowman with James
Key-rings
Height   7½in (6.5cm)
Introduced   1994

TSUKAMOTO
Snowman Standing
Snowman and James in Forest
James Hugging Snowman
Snowman detail
Key-rings musical
Height   1½in (4cm)
Introduced   1994

Wooden musical jewellery box
Height   2¾in (7cm)
Introduced   1990

Cardboard music box
Height   2in (5cm)
Introduced   1990

Star clock
Height   4in (10cm)
Introduced   1994 (see page 51)

Zot Japan
Introduced   1998
Withdrawn   1999

Key Chain watch LCD
Animation watch LCD
Watch – not illustrated

Touchpon light.

Fridge magnets and key-rings.

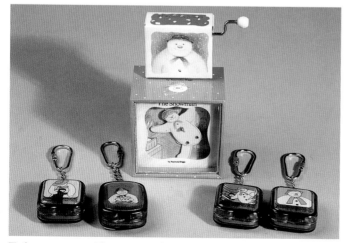

Tsukamoto musical key-rings and music boxes.

PVC money box.

KITCHENWARES

Electric fan
Personal electric fan
Ice cream maker with handle
Electric ice crusher
Thermal mug
Thermal ice cream cup
Thermos flask
Hot cushion
Introduced   1997 onwards

Deep metal pan
Milk pan
Metal pot
Metal mug
Saucepan
Frying pan
Cheese fondue set
Introduced   1997 onwards

Plastic containers and canteens
Introduced   2003

Cooler bags
Introduced   2003

Fridge air freshener
Introduced   2003

Ice makers.

Lunch-boxes
Various sizes and designs
Introduced   1989 onwards

Plastic tumblers
Various designs
Introduced   1993 and 1994

Melamine mug
Pink and blue
Introduced   1993

Jug
Introduced   1998

Lunch cloths – various designs
Lunch bags – various designs
Introduced   1989 onwards

Tea cosy, hot grips, oven glove
Introduced   1990

Enamel pots and pans.

Christmas cake candles
Figurative candles
Introduced 1992 onwards

CUTLERY

Fork and Spoon set
Green, orange and blue plastic
Introduced 1989

Fork and Spoon set
Plastic handles
Introduced 1990

Spoon set – three spoons
Introduced 1993

BATHROOM AND BEDROOM

Brush stand – three designs
Dust box – three designs
Introduced 1999

Toothbrush, toothpaste and mug
Introduced 1993

Snowman soaps and soapbubbles
Introduced 1991

Lip gloss and mascara
Introduced 1998

Mirror – two designs
Introduced 1989

Cosmetic bags
Introduced 1995

Towels
Variety of sizes and designs
Introduced 1989 onwards

Bath mat and toilet seat cover
Introduced 1989 onwards

Handkerchiefs
Introduced 1989 onwards

Cushions
Introduced 1989 onwards

Bed-mats
Introduced 1989 onwards

Quilt covers, sheets and curtains
Introduced 1999

Blanket, lamp, roomshoes
Introduced 2003

Plastic lunch boxes, tumblers and cutlery.

Designs for figurative candles

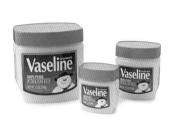

Vaseline.

Designs for dust boxes.

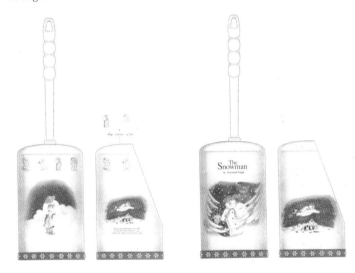

Designs for brush stands.

STATIONERY AND WRITING MATERIALS

Tins for pencils etc
Various shapes and sizes
Introduced   1989 onwards

Mechanical pencils, pens and
rulers and erasers in same designs
Pens and correction pens
Introduced   1989 onwards

Plastic pencil cases and bags
Introduced   1992 onwards

Drawing sets, sketch pads, exercise
books, address books, notebooks,
stationery sets, pencil sets, erasers,
calendars
Introduced   1989 onwards

Stationery.

Writing materials and holders.

Plastic case.

Jigsaw.

Sekiguchi soft toys.

Sekiguchi soft toys.

Also jotters, binders, envelopes, photo albums
Introduced 1992 onwards

TOYS AND GAMES

Soft Toys
Snowman in various sizes
Snowman Dressed Up
Snowman with Balloons
Introduced 1989 onwards

Bean bags
Soft key-rings
Rattles
Soft rucksacks
Christmas stocking
Introduced 1989 onwards

Wooden toys
Introduced 2003

Jigsaw Puzzles
252, 315 and 550 pieces

Mini puzzles
Introduced 1989
Jigsaw puzzles

108, 300 and 1,000 pieces
Introduced 1996

Jigsaw in tin – four designs
Introduced 2000

Die-cut mobiles
Fridge magnets
Introduced 1989 onwards

CLOTHES

Sweat shirts
T-shirts
Pyjamas
Slippers
Socks
Hats
Scarf
Aprons
PVC bags
Introduced 1989 onwards

SEGA ENTERPRISES
GLASS

Snowman Sledging
Snowman Flying
Snowman and James on Motorbike
Snowman and Penguins
Snowman Accordion
Frosted glass tumblers – five designs
Height $4^{1}/_{4}$in (11cm)
Introduced 2000

Notes
Balloons
Snowflakes
Frosted glass plates – three designs
Diameter   6in (15cm)
Introduced 2001

Notes
Balloons
Snowflakes
Frosted glass goblets – three designs
Height $4^{1}/_{2}$in (11.5cm)
Introduced 2001

Sega tumblers.

Sega tumblers and plates.

Sega water globes.

Sega clocks.

Snowman Flying
Snowman Sitting
James Hugging Snowman
Snowman Dancing
Snowman with Star
Water globes – five designs
Height   3¹/₂in (9cm)
Introduced 1999
Made in China
18,000 of these were produced

CERAMICS

Snowman and James Dancing
**Snowman and James Flying -
detail**
**Snowman and James Flying with
Snowmen**
Snowman face – detail
**Snowman and James with
Balloons**
Mugs – five designs
Made in China
Height   3¹/₄in (8cm)
Introduced 2000

Sega mugs.

Sega metal charms.

Snowman and James at Christmas Tree 2000
Snowman and James Flying 2001
Snowman and James with Christmas Cake 2000
Clocks – three designs
Diameter   6in (15cm)
Introduced   2000

Snowman Head and Snowflake
Snowman Dancing and Note
Snowman Standing and Snowflake
Snowman Flying and Star
Charms – four pairs
Height   1in (2.5cm)
Introduced   2000

PLASTIC

Snowman
Christmas Tree
White, green and blue
Height   8in (20.5cm)
Introduced   2001

Snowman with Star
Snowman Hugging James
Money bank – two designs
Introduced   1999

Sega Christmas trees and key-rings.

Snowman with Star (blue)
Snowman Sitting (yellow)
Snowman Dressing Up (green)
Snowman Standing (blue)
Wind chimes– four designs
Height   9in (23cm)
Introduced 1999

Lantern, revolving – three designs
Height   5¹/₄in (13.5cm)
Introduced 1999

Tea Serving Sets – four designs
Teapots and cups
Green, blue, yellow and red
Introduced 1999
15,000 sets were made – teacup
had defective handle

Sega wind chimes.

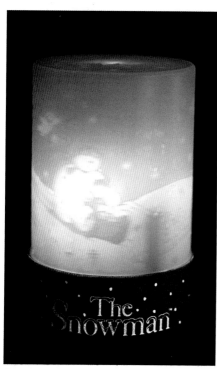

Sega revolving lantern.

Designs for Sega money boxes.

Sega photo stickers.

92

Sega tea serving sets.

Taito wreaths.

Sega soft toy.

Snowman
Soft toy
Height   9¼in (24cm)
Introduced 2001

TAITO
Plastic globe lights – three designs
Green, red and blue
Height   6¾in (17cm)
Introduced 2002
Not illustrated

Christmas wreaths – four designs
Introduced 2002

Snowman soft toy
Not illustrated

JAPANESE LICENCE HOLDERS
PAST AND PRESENT

Towel display in a Japanese store.

Over the years a large number of Japanese companies have held a licence from Sony Plaza to make Snowman merchandise for the Japanese market.

Art Print Japan
Postcards and greetings cards

Azuma
Ceramics and glass, tableware and bathroom accessories

Bandai
Capsule game, cosmetics, candles

Beverly
Puzzles, stickers and stamps

Daiwa International
Pins and badges

Doshima
Enamel cookware

Doushisya
Housewares

Dreams Come True
Illuminated tree

Epoch
Jigsaws

Fuji
Enamel pots and pans

Gakken Toy Hobby
Postcards

Hakuhodo
Promotion of Takano's social welfare related products

Hanix
Toothbrushes, mugs

Hasebe
Fastener accessories, straps, pin badges and mascots

Insist
Blankets and bedcovers

I-Planet
Advertisement for Mitsubishi Electric

Itochu
Soft furnishings for bedrooms and bathrooms

Iword
New Year's card printing

Kamika
Stationery and paper products

Kokka
Clothes

Kowa
Women's clothes

Mainichi Kokokusha
Advertising for Agency of Natural Resources and Energy

M&M
Telephone cards, stationery

MTI
Mobile phone images

Nihon Record Fukyu
Music gift card vouchers

Nishi-Nippon Bank
Print work from Toppan Printing Company

Ogiwara
Men's pyjamas and underwear

Okamoto
Socks, stockings and leggings

Okina
Travel toiletries

Parco
Calendars

Re-Ment
Mobile phone straps

Saitou Confectionery
Cakes and biscuits

Sega Enterprises
Premium products for games

Sekiguchi
Soft toys

Tachibana Textile Fabrics
Blanket, vest

Taito
Premium products for games

Takaishi
Bags and wallets

Takara
Infants' and children's clothes

Takashimaya
Plastic cup

Tokin
Customized telephone card

Tokyu Hands
Premium goods for Coca Cola
Japan

RP Topra
Cooler flasks

Toppan Printing
Sales promotion for
Nishi-Nippon Bank

Tsukamoto
Musical boxes

Uchino
Towels, bathroom accessories,
bath robes, table linens,
kitchen accessories

Utsumi Sangyo
Premium products for
commercial use

Wing Corporation
Touchpon light, jigsaws

Wise
Fashion stickers
Switch plate seals

Yamaka Shoten
Ceramic tableware and giftware

Yogetsu
Stationery and writing
materials

Zels
Clothes

Zot Japan
Watches

KOREA

Imax
Socks and gloves

Luke International
Underwear

TAIWAN
Hsinex International
Premiums for International
Bank of Taipei

A bedroom featuring a range of The Snowman clothes and soft furnishings.

UK, Europe and US Licence Holders Past and Present

Abella
Knitwear

Addis
Wisdom toothbrushes

Animated Displays
Animated scenes and figures for hire

Armstrong and Claydon
Household tins

Atlas Lace Paper
Paper partyware

Avana Bakeries
Party cake for Marks and Spencer

Babygro
Baby sleepwear for Marks and Spencer

Barnsley Canister
Tin boxes

Bear, Bear and Bear
Cake decorating candles for Lakeland Plastics

BMP DDB
Volkswagen advertisement

Board Buddies
Cardboard cut outs. Did not proceed.

Book Tokens
Book token wallets

Border Fine Arts
Enamel boxes

Borders Group
Pre-paid gift cards

Bradford Exchange
Christmas tree ornaments. Tested but not produced

BSB
Bags, napkins, puzzles, stationery

Burford Garden Centre
Christmas grotto

Caltime
Advent calendars and card holders

Candlepower
Shaped candles

CBS Records
LP and tape of sound track

Childline
Fund raising badges and stationery

Churchill Square Shopping Centre
Christmas decorations

Cloverleaf
Clock for Marks and Spencer

Compton & Woodhouse
Wall plates. Limited production for test market.

Copywrite Stationery
Gift stationery

Country Artists
Crystal laser sculptures

Courtaulds Leisurewear
Baby bodysuits

Creative Cake Company
Party cake, cup cakes, mini rolls for Tesco

Creative Confectionery
Chocolate, sugar, jelly and candy confectionery

Crummles
Enamel boxes

David Halsall
Carousel fan lights.

Dawson Rogers
Nursery bedding

Deeko
Paper partyware

Delgado
Christmas crackers for Toys R Us

Donovan and Hanson
Children's clothes

Downpace
Adult slippers

Eden Toys
Soft toys, slippers, melamine

Elgin Court Designs
Greetings cards, gift wrap

Fine Art Development
Christmas crackers

Fort James
Kitchen towel

HC Ford
Flock figures

Frankel and Roth
Bags

Gemma International
Greetings cards, wrap and party invitations

Gilchrist Confectionery
Chocolates

Golden Bear
Soft toys, mobiles, puppets

Goulds
Tissues, kitchen towels, toilet tissue

Grosvenor of London
Toiletries

Guild of China and Glass Retailers
Steiff Snowman

Hallmark Cards Tigerprint Division
Greetings cards, wrap and tags for Marks and Spencer

Hamilton-McBride
Bedding

Hamish Hamilton
The original book and board books

Hamleys
Christmas window displays

Hammicks
Christmas cards

Hestair Hope
Jigsaw puzzles

Highbridge/Faber Music
Full score, piano sheet music

Horizon Biscuit Company
Shaped biscuits

Hotcakes (formerly Elite Gift Boxes)
Cracker tin

House Martin (later Spearmark)
Clocks

Icarus Company
Metal play tray, waste bin, plastic mats

Fritz Wegner illustrations for *The Better Brown Stories* by Allan Ahlberg from Raymond Briggs' collection.

Intarsia
Knitting patterns

International Christmas
Christmas goods

International Greetings
Christmas crackers, gift wrap, tags and cards for Boots

Jacobsens - Intergoods Bakery
Chocolate chip cookies in tins

Jamont
Kitchen towels

Keith Butters
Porcelain plant pots for Tesco

Kidstamps
Rubber stamps

Kinetic Enterprises
Toiletries

Kinnerton Confectionery
Chocolate Snowman products

Kitty Little
Fragrant characters

Kleinert's
Blanket sleepers, bibs and fleece garments

Lakefield Marketing
Christmas cards, paper, hat, scarf and mitten set for Peter Rabbit and Friends

Lister
Rugs

Maid Marian Bakeries (Inter-link Foods) Party cakes

Manuscript
Framed pictures

Marcel Schurman
Christmas cards, bags, tins

MBI
Wedgwood bone china plates for direct marketing by Danbury Mint
Tested but not produced

M & F Jinks
Shaped slippers and muff

Milling and Baking Products
Shaped biscuit and book set

Steve Bell illustration for the cover of *Private Eye* from Raymond Briggs' collection.

Moore USA
Mailing for American Lung Association

Multiple Sound
Book and cassette pack

Murdoch Books
Cross stitch charts

Nicholas & Harris
Cakes

Obpacher Verlag
Postcards and cards

Palace Video
Home video film

Paper House Productions
Magnets, stickers, notecards, photo cards

Pic Toys
Board games, stencil and painting kits

Polygram
Videos

Prestige Toys
Soft toys, slippers, melamine

Puffin Books
Paperback of The Snowman

Quicksilver Games
Cassette tape

Ragged Robin Designs
Cross stitch kits Leslie Norah Hills

Rainbow Designs
Badges, mirrors, stickers, tinware
Distributor of soft toys for Prestige Toys

Redan
Snowman magazine

Robert Frederick
Art sets, photo albums, games, place mats, gift boxes

Robin Wools
Knitting patterns

Royal Doulton
Ceramic, crystal and enamel gifts

Salisbury Candle Company
Candles

Scandinavian Designs
Wrapping paper and bows

Schwedt and Gesing
Tins

Scorpio Products
Nursery stickers

Shapes
Acrylic mobiles

Shreds
PVC aprons, bags and pencil cases

Sight and Sound Animations
In store displays of animated figures and scenes

Silvestri
Music boxes and water globes

Sirdar
Instructions and charts for knitwear

Sowa and Reiser
Etchings

Studio Art
Limited edition reproductions from the film

Supercast
Plaster and candle moulding sets

Susan Prescot Games
Jigsaws, board games

Swan Mill Paper Products
Paper partyware

Swico
Raymond Weil
Did not proceed

Tie Rack Trading
Men's ties, socks and boxer shorts

Timothy Lawrence
Children's slippers and boots

Unique Images
Disposable partyware, Christmas crackers

United Biscuits
Snowman shaped frozen dessert

Van den Bergh Foods
Flora margarine promotion

View-Master
3 D film reels

Waterford Wedgwood/ Coalport
Ceramic ware

Westland Giftware
Water globe

Westminster Collection
First day covers

William Briggs
Longstitch kits

Zeppelin Balloons
Silver foil balloons

Raymond Briggs and the author, Louise Irvine, discussing The Snowman.

FURTHER READING

The Snowman
Raymond Briggs, Hamish Hamilton 1978

Raymond Briggs Blooming Books
Nicolette Jones, Jonathan Cape London 2003

Royal Doulton Cartoon Classics and other
Character Figures
Louise Irvine, UK International Ceramics 1998

Charlton Standard Catalogue of Royal Doulton
Storybook Figurines
Jean Dale with introduction by Louise Irvine,
7th edition, The Charlton Press 2003

WEBSITES OF INTEREST

www.thesnowman.co.uk
www.charactergifts.com/thesnowman

www.coalport-snowman.co.uk

USEFUL ADDRESSES

Copyrights
Merchandise Agents for Writers and Artists
23 West Bar
Banbury
Oxfordshire OX16 9SA
www.copyrights.co.uk
Tel: 01295 672050
Fax: 01295 672060

Hamish Hamilton
80 The Strand
London WC2R 0RL
Tel: 020 7010 3000
Fax: 020 7010 6060

Sony Plaza
International Trade Division
Sony Building
5-3-1 Ginza
Chuo-ku, Tokyo 104
Japan
www.sonyplaza.com

The Snowman Newsletter
Contact Alex Tham
General Manager
Snowman Enterprises
39 Grafton Way
London W1T 5DE
Tel: 020 7388 2222 ext 217
Fax: 020 7383 4192
e-mail: alex.tham@btconnect.com